An Outback Nurse

THEA HAYES

ALLEN&UNWIN
SYDNEY • MELBOURNE • AUCKLAND • LONDON

First published in 2014

Copyright © Thea Hayes 2014

Allen & Unwin
83 Alexander Street
Crows Nest NSW 2065
Australia
Phone: (61 2) 8425 0100
Email: info@allenandunwin.com
Web: www.allenandunwin.com

Cataloguing-in-Publication details are available
from the National Library of Australia
www.trove.nla.gov.au

ISBN 978 1 76011 132 8

Cover design by Darian Causby
Set in 13/18.5 pt Berkeley Oldstyle by Midland Typesetters, Australia
Printed and bound in Australia by Griffin Press

10 9 8 7 6 5 4 3 2 1

Foreword

Congratulations to Thea Hayes for writing this fine book and to Allen & Unwin for publishing it. Far too often, the people with the 'real' stories to tell get passed over by publishers on the grounds that they are not known, or 'might not find a market'. I know from personal experience that there is an audience out there that craves the genuine article. I also know that the best advertising is still word-of-mouth. So I predict that *Outback Nurse* will go very well. I hope so.

Thea represents those many 'bush women' who have done it tough, have known privation and disappointment, have had to work long and often thankless hours without the back-up and assistance they deserve as a result of the loneliness in which their lives are led. But they have known loneliness only in terms of vast distance, for the family lives they have created are indeed joyful, productive and not to be swapped, no matter what the circumstance. Laughter is an essential component. I wrote about them in my poem 'Bush Woman':

She's the backbone of this country
She's alive and well today
She's the mainstay of Australia
And that's all there is to say

Thea brought security to many lives through her dedication to the people of the Outback, as a nurse and as a kindly, generous wife on one of Australia's biggest and most famous cattle stations, Wave Hill. She is the widow of Ralph, one of the great cattlemen. They had to be tough, resolute people, but the rigours of their lives were softened by the level of fair play that they sought to impose on all situations. There is no better example than in the famous 'strikes' at Wave Hill. Thea and Ralph had to take particular managerial stances in those troubled days, but at all times they showed their respect for the Aboriginal people that they had known from childhood and with whom they had shared the responsibility of running the station effectively and productively over so many years.

I know that the 'bushies' will love this book and I hope it sells by the thousands.

Ted Egan AO
Alice Springs

Contents

Contents

To the memory of Ralph Hayes and to the many people of the Outback, both white and Aboriginal, who contributed to the lifestyle that made this book possible.

Preface

The Northern Territory Outback is mostly a wide brown land with vast expanses of desert where spinifex grows: a sunburnt country. Then there are the rich pastures that extend on flat black soil plains for miles towards the horizon. Rugged mountain ranges and huge monoliths reach for the sky, interspersed with gorges gashed out of rocks from thousands of years of wind and rain.

The first inhabitants of this beautiful but harsh land were the Aboriginal people, believed to have been here since the Ice Age, around fifty to seventy thousand years ago. These nomads treated the country well as they saw the land as an extension of themselves. Hunting and gathering, they lived on yams, berries, grubs, grasses, fish and native animals.

When white men came with their cattle to the centre of Australia, life for the Aboriginal people changed forever. Existing on the outskirts of the huge stations, they gradually became involved in the workings of the cattle industry, losing in the process a great part of their nomadic lifestyle and culture.

It was in this vastness that I found myself as a young nurse. The Northern Territory was to give me a home with more love in it than I ever expected. And, also unexpectedly, this vast land was to be the backdrop for one of the most momentous struggles in the fight for equality of the Australian Aboriginal people.

1

Sydney, Australia

1959

I was coming home after a year of adventure overseas: living and working in London, hitchhiking around Europe with my friends, and returning via the United States and Canada, where I had visited my adventurous brother Tim in Vancouver. Tim had settled there when he'd taken a job with a surveying firm, and he and his Australian fiancée, Faye, drove me to the harbour in their car, festooned with yellow and green streamers and cut-out kangaroos.

SS *Lakemba* didn't look too bad, and was larger than I'd expected. It was a less than state-of-the-art freighter carrying eight cash-strapped passengers, plus crew, and laden with timber. We were meant to set sail at 12.30 p.m., but visitors still being on board ruined that. There was frantic waving and screaming from all as the crew attempted to depart on time.

The trip back from Canada was slow. The *Lakemba* chugged away for eleven days before arriving in Honolulu, where we stayed for only one day, much to our disappointment. A few of us managed to do a quick tour of the town, ending up at the Royal Hawaiian Hotel sipping whisky sours on their patio beside Waikiki Beach. Too divine for words.

On to Suva where the crew unloaded their timber: this was to take three days, so a group of us hired a car and spent an exciting time at Korolevu Bay, on the western coast of Fiji. We danced every night in a thatch-roofed beach-side nightclub. With the right company it could have been very romantic, but this was a group intent on getting home rather than forging lifelong relationships. However, the sweet sounds of a traditional Tongan orchestra did not go wasted on travellers who were experiencing their last taste of exotica before returning to staid 1950s Australia.

Next stop: Sydney.

It was a glorious day in March when the *Lakemba* sailed into Sydney. As we steered past the coast's spectacular heads, I viewed the most beautiful harbour in the world. How fortunate I felt to be an Australian, and particularly to be home. I was excited at the thought of seeing my mother again, and eager to catch up with my boyfriend, Colin, whom I'd met a year before leaving Australia. Colin was a civil engineer, a gorgeous guy and a conservative type, often wearing a tweed jacket and smoking a pipe.

But I was also a little anxious. Would Colin still feel the same way about me after a year's absence? And would I feel the same about him?

After the ship docked I soon found myself in Colin's arms. It was both thrilling and strangely uncomfortable.

Several days later when he invited me to dinner I found out why our reunion did not feel right. My gorgeous Colin had metamorphosed into my heartbreaker: he'd shifted his attentions elsewhere while I'd been overseas. I was broken-hearted and cried on my mother's shoulder, but at least I was home. *Damn it*, I thought, *why did I come back so early?* I could have still been overseas with my friends.

I quickly decided that I'd best get over this dismal period and do a course. I was accepted into the Crown Street Women's Hospital in Surry Hills, Sydney, for the twelve-month Certificate in Obstetrics, beginning in August.

About twenty of us, all registered nurses, started together. We thought we knew everything, but at Crown Street we found we knew nothing. As trainee midwives we were not allowed even to test a wee without having it checked by a superior. However, we coped with being put down by the registered midwives who, despite us having completed four years of nursing training, treated us as if we were ignorant. We took it in turns with the medical students to do our fifteen mandatory deliveries.

In my last six weeks at Crown Street I decided I'd had enough of hospital work. Carefully, I read all the positions in *The Sydney Morning Herald* for double-certificated nursing sisters that were not in a hospital, looking for that perfect job, applying for several potentials.

One evening I had a phone call from Wylva, a friend I'd met overseas and with whom I'd shared a flat in Kensington, London. 'I'm going on a trip to Ayres Rock and Alice Springs. Why don't you come with me?' she suggested. 'It's being organised by students from the CSIRO research division—they'll do the driving.'

'That sounds great, what date do you leave?' I asked, as I still had another three weeks to complete my course.

'Not until the end of the month.'

'Wonderful,' I said, 'I'll be finished two days before.' *I can always look for that special job when I get back*, I thought to myself.

When I graduated it was time to farewell the friends and classmates with whom I'd lived and worked for the past twelve months. We all exchanged addresses and phone numbers, and promised to keep in touch. Everyone wished me well on my trip to Ayres Rock. My reply: 'I'll be back in three or four weeks. I will ring you then.'

In my two free days before the trip, I moved to a shared three-bedroom flat in Edgecliff, not far from some close friends in Darling Point. I didn't unpack. I put together a small suitcase of clothes, then rang my mother in Wollongong.

'Any mail, Mum?' I asked.

'Yes, darling, a letter from the Australian Investment Agency.'

'Have I really?' I asked, taken by surprise. 'I applied for a job with them, weeks ago, but it was for a triple-certificated nurse, at least twenty-five years old. And you'll never guess where it is: a cattle station in the Northern Territory. Quick, please read out the letter.'

Sydney, Australia

The letter was from a Mr Alan Perry, the company secretary, and said that the Australian Investment Agency would very much like to interview me.

I considered it and decided that as I didn't have much to do before we left, and I'd already packed, why not have an interview with this Mr Alan Perry? I thought the property could be just outside Alice Springs, or even on the way to Ayres Rock. Wylva and I could probably be taken out there. How exciting! We'd be able to see a real live cattle station in the Northern Territory.

2

The interview

Having rung to say I was on my way, I caught a taxi to the Australian Investment Agency. It was upstairs on George Street, just above the entrance to Wynyard Station.

I didn't have to wait long before I was ushered into Mr Alan Perry's office. I was feeling quite nervous, as I was there under a pretext: I'd only come for the interview because I was curious to see an Outback cattle station.

Mr Perry stood when I entered the room. He was a fairly short, well-dressed gentleman with a warm, welcoming smile that made me feel completely at ease.

'How do you do, Thea? Do sit down,' he said, indicating a chair. 'So, you're interested in going to Wave Hill Station as the nursing sister?'

'Well, yes,' I said hesitantly, 'but I'm about to leave on a trip to Alice Springs and Ayres Rock, so I'll soon know more about the area.'

'I'll tell you about Wave Hill,' he began. 'It's a large cattle station, the second-largest property in the world under one management. It has an area of six thousand square miles or about four million acres, and is situated about five hundred miles north-west of Alice.'

There goes Wylva's and my firsthand viewing of a cattle station, I thought.

'So who owns Wave Hill, Mr Perry?' I asked.

'The Vesteys, one of the richest aristocratic families in Britain. They've built up a worldwide empire: they've got interests in property development, grocery wholesaling, supermarkets, insurance and travel, and they own shipping lines and wool mills, and cattle properties in Queensland, the Northern Territory and Western Australia, as well as in Brazil. They're the world's biggest producer and retailer of meat. Lord Vestey died a few years ago and his young grandson Sam has inherited his title.'

Wow! I thought. *Wave Hill is sounding very interesting.*

'The manager is Tom Fisher, who's worked for the Vestey Company for many years: an excellent manager. He was recently divorced from his second wife, which means the nursing sister must also be housekeeper and hostess, as Wave Hill receives many visitors.'

'The job sounds fascinating. How many people live at Wave Hill?'

'There are thirty whites and 240 Aborigines on the station. You certainly won't get bored. In fact, I'm sure you'll love it up there.'

'What about women? Are there any white women?'

'Yes, the mechanic and the bookkeeper both have wives.'

He sounded so keen to hire me that I started to panic. How could I refuse, when he was being so helpful?

'Mr Perry,' I began, 'I'm afraid I haven't got three certificates. I've only got my general nursing and midwifery, and you did advertise for a triple-certificated nursing sister.'

'I don't think we'll worry about that,' he said with a smile.

My heart sank. 'You also wanted someone over twenty-five,' I tried again.

'Oh! That's perfectly all right. You're obviously a very competent nurse, so what's a year or two?'

Oh dear, I'm not getting out of this very well, I thought. All my friends from my course and overseas trip lived in Sydney, and I suddenly realised I didn't want to leave. We'd shared a wonderful time, and I envisaged the fun ahead.

So what on earth was I doing being interviewed for a job in the middle of the Northern Territory?

3

My early adventures

My mother, Nancie Osborne, started her nursing training at the Royal Prince Alfred Hospital in Sydney. There, two years later, she met and fell in love with the handsome William McGovern, a brave ex–soldier.

My father had grown up on a Black Mountain farm in the New England district of New South Wales, and at the age of eighteen had enlisted with the Australian Imperial Forces in Armidale on 3 April 1916. A month later, with the 36th Battalion, he sailed off on HMAT *Beltana* to Gallipoli. He was a corporal, then a second lieutenant. After being wounded and transferred back to England to recuperate, he was sent to officer school at Oxford, receiving his commission as lieutenant. Later he was wounded again in Messines, France, and finally came home at the end of the war.

My parents were married at St Mary's Cathedral in Sydney. After they went on a golfing honeymoon, Dad was posted with the Commonwealth Bank of Australia to Wagga Wagga, where my two older brothers, Tony and Tim, were born. My family then moved to Albury, a large town in the Riverina district on the New South Wales/Victorian border, and Dad managed a bank branch there. I and my younger brother, Terry, were born in Albury some years later, before my family moved once more, this time to Melbourne. When World War II started, Dad joined up again, now as Captain McGovern. In 1942, he insisted that we be evacuated to stay with his mother in the small town of Guyra, New South Wales, because of the fear of a Japanese invasion. That same year, two Japanese mini-submarines came into Sydney Harbour.

Dad was killed in a traffic accident in Melbourne that September. He was only forty-six. My poor mother. I was six years old and Terry was four. Tony and Tim were fourteen and twelve. Tony ended up leaving school soon after Dad's death, and worked for an accountant to help Mum with family finances.

I can only remember seeing my father once; I suppose I was too young to remember the other times. In Wollongong, on route to Guyra, Dad came up from Melbourne to farewell his family. I was in bed and unwell with an infected foot, and he stood at the end of my bed. I was probably crying. I can't remember him giving me a cuddle, but I'm sure he did.

We had one year in Guyra. It was the first time I saw snow. Oh, and it was *so* cold. I loved the small-town atmosphere; everyone knew everyone. Every Saturday afternoon, the whole town went shopping down the main street. We kids would be given three pence and it would take us all afternoon to spend it. One penny's worth of this, half a penny's worth of that, a penny ice-cream which we ate while we took turns on the swings in the park.

After our time in Guyra, my family moved to Wollongong to be near my maternal grandmother, and that's where I grew up. We had a very happy childhood and adolescence there. Garc, as we called my grandmother, had moved to Wollongong from Milton after the death of my grandfather, and married a lovely man named George Allen. (Not to be confused with *the* George Allen, the founder of Allen & Unwin, who married my great-great-aunt Anne Eliza.) Garc and her George owned a large colonial house that had been divided into two flats: we lived in one and they in the other.

There was a line of coral trees with bright-red flowers down the driveway, leading to a huge backyard. Garden beds of flowers and vegetables were scattered around the back lawn, and at the bottom of the garden there was a chookyard, Uncle George's pride and joy. Every day he would take the food scraps from our chook bins and ceremoniously mix them with pollard. This feed mix had such a delicious smell, I thought I could eat it. Never did, though! We kids loved to go with Uncle George to feed the hens and rooster. We'd watch him pick up a broody hen and lock her in a special cage, with her own nest for laying and setting the eggs.

We even had a well in our backyard that was covered with a cement lid about two inches thick. One day when the lid had been pushed back, my four-year-old brother fell inside. Luckily there was water at the bottom and it wasn't too deep.

Tim had to climb down a ladder to rescue Terry, and thankfully he was okay.

I started school at Saint Francis Xavier Girls' Convent, taught by the Good Samaritan Sisters. Some were lovely; one was a monster. When I was in sixth class one of the sisters decided I was to sit for a bursary to help with my education expenses. Every time I had a mathematical sum wrong, 'Out here, Thea McGovern,' she would say.

As I stood nervously in front of the class, the sister would crack me across the hand with a long stick while she sat poised on her throne. I hated her. I told my mother about her. But of course nothing was done. No parents complained to schools about their mode of discipline in those days.

I was an adventurous type, having grown up with three brothers and having a best friend, Nellie, who was as adventurous as me. We were ten years of age and went to school together at the convent. Every weekend, after my ballet classes, we would find something exciting to do.

We'd climb Mount Keira, at the back of Wollongong, and swing on the monkey vines hanging from the trees, have a picnic on a different beach or in a different park along the South Coast every few weeks, camp in my backyard in a tent, go doubling all over town on my big brother's bike, take the train to Sydney and walk across the Harbour Bridge, or go to the museum or the art gallery—or, in summer, just go to the beach every day. Life was safer in those days. Kids were free to roam without their parents.

*

When my mother met my father, she thought, *Blow nursing*, and married him after only two years of her training. Back then when a girl married she was expected to give up her career and become a housewife. Spinsters, as single women were called, were the only women who could continue working.

'Now, Thea,' Mum would say to me, 'I think you should become a nurse and continue where I left off.'

So that's how I had the vision to become a nurse. However, it was touch and go for a while. I'd wanted to become a ballerina. Growing up in Wollongong, every Thursday and Friday afternoon and Saturday morning I attended the Enid Hall School of Ballet. I loved it and did an exam each year: tap, toe and ballet. We also put on an annual concert in the movie theatre, performing two or three routines. I longed to be a ballerina, but it was even more difficult in the 1950s than it is now, especially for a young woman in Wollongong. And there weren't many other career choices for women, with nursing, teaching, stenography and university as the main options.

Then Nellie said, 'Come to teachers college with me! My sisters tell me that everyone has a ball.'

Having put in an application, I went with Nellie to a seminar in Sydney for those interested in becoming primary school-teachers. After the leaving results came out, I also applied to Royal Prince Alfred Hospital—where my mother had trained—to become a registered nurse. I had the interview and was told they would soon let me know the result. In the meantime I received a letter of acceptance to Bathurst Teachers College, plus a train ticket. I kept asking myself, *What should I do?*

I waited and the following week was accepted at Royal Prince Alfred, and I have never regretted that decision. After four years of general nursing training, I went home to live with my family in Wollongong. Having applied to the local hospital for a position, I was offered sister-in-charge of Isolation. Confident about my nursing skills, I happily accepted.

But all I wanted to do was travel overseas. I went to my cousin Gwen's wedding in Guyra. In those days girls had a 'glory box': a collection of linen, doilies, pot holders, and anything else that would be required when they got married. Gwen had set up her glory box in her mother's, my aunt's, house. Every room was full of glory box stuff, and the whole town came for an inspection.

Auntie Kate said to me, 'Wouldn't you love to have all this?'

'Oh yes, Auntie Kate, how I would love to—and if I did, I would sell the lot and go to England.'

My aunt was horrified.

For nine months I worked full time while saving all my wages to go to London with one of my Wollongong friends, Jill Askew. Together we babysat, cleaned cars and had a fun social life with a great crowd of friends who, like us, had come home to Wollongong to work after completing their courses in Sydney.

It was the rock and roll era, and we partied on at anyone's home when their parents were away for the evening. I met Colin at one of these parties.

Jill and I sailed for London on the Cunard ship the *Orontes*. Most ocean liners had two classes: first in the upper decks and second down below. Our ship just had one class, but we were still in its bowels, on 'H' deck, because we wanted to save our money for Europe.

In the dining room we met a lovely girl, Anne Smidlin, nicknamed Smiddy, and the three of us became great friends during the five weeks it took to get to London via the Suez Canal. We stopped in Melbourne, Adelaide, Perth, Naples, Marseille and Gibraltar, and arrived in England on Anzac Day. That was the start of an absolutely fantastic year with the most wonderful companions, travelling around England and Europe.

The 'in thing' to do, so we'd heard before leaving Australia, was to hire a London cab to tour the Continent. So, of course, that's what we planned to do, until we caught up with a nursing mate of mine in London, who said, 'You can't hire a London cab. It's far too expensive. The thing to do is hitchhike.'

'What?!' we all moaned.

'Don't worry,' she said, 'I'll go with you, and then we'll have two pairs, easier for hitching.' Three was sometimes considered too many, and two pairs meant you could go in two cars. Well, that seemed to be her thinking, anyway.

Once this was decided, we had to obtain membership of the Backpacker and Hostel Association, and buy our bed sheets, backpacks and other necessities. Finally we were ready. We rang my friend, only to discover that she hadn't thought we were serious—and there was no way she could leave with us.

Shocked, we decided it would have to be just the three of us, and we hoped our drivers wouldn't mind. Actually, we felt much safer with three in a car.

Our trip started with a ferry ride from England to Ostend, Belgium, where we caught a train to Bruges, the sweetest little fairytale town, with cobbled streets, quaint shops and a statue of Our Lady at every second corner. We found our first youth hostel: two hundred beds, very modern. We were almost ready to jump under the shower when we discovered there was only one tap. This was April in Europe, akin to the middle of winter in New South Wales. We had our showers amid continuous screams, but I must admit we felt amazing afterwards.

Next day we were out on the road. Who was going to do that thumb sign first? 'Not me!' we all cried. Finally, having noted a small truck coming towards us, I plucked up enough courage to signal the driver. He stopped. The truck reeked of fish. Our very obliging driver indicated that one woman should go in the front and two in the back with the stinking tarps and nets. We didn't care. We had our first lift and thought our driver was wonderful.

What followed was a succession of fascinating, personality-plus drivers, ranging from a handsome middle-aged Italian in his Mercedes, who took us all out to dine in Ravenna; a truckie who produced a bottle of Rhine wine as we drove along the river Rhine; and a racing-car driver who wanted to take me to see the lights of Rome, and with whom I reluctantly went after being pushed into it by my 'mates'.

He picked me up at the youth hostel in his Lamborghini, and we observed the lights of Rome from one of the seven hills that form the ancient city's geographical heart. Unfortunately he wasn't as good-looking as his car, couldn't speak English and was trying to be romantic. Every time he started to put his arm around my shoulder, I would start asking him questions in broken schoolgirl French. He knew as much French as I did, and as he stumbled to answer he would forget about his arm. Eventually he got sick of it, and me, and took me back to the hostel.

In Rome I applied for a nanny position. Jill had procured a job with an Italian family, teaching English, so I thought I'd do something similar. I was picked up by a chauffeur-driven BMW and taken to a beautiful mansion on the Appian Way. Here I was interviewed by Signor Lollobridgida—the husband of Gina Lollobridgida, the Italian film star—in a gorgeous, classically designed room, while I sat on a luxurious pink velvet lounge. Of course he wanted someone to stay for two years, and it wouldn't have been fair to stay for a couple of months and then leave. I had too much more to see on the Continent, so I declined the job and left. But I was thrilled with the experience of meeting someone famous.

On my return to London, after a fantastic two months hitchhiking around the Continent, it was time to get a job. I didn't want to work as a nurse; I wanted to try other types of employment, so I joined a casual work agency and went to Swan & Edgar, a large department store in Piccadilly Circus, to sell ladies' suits.

It was sale time and summertime in London. The suits were winter quality and horrid. Some customers would put one on and ask, 'What do you think?' I tried to give positive responses but it was very difficult as they looked ghastly no matter who tried them on. Somehow I managed to sell fifteen, so I was asked to stay on. *No way!* It was the standing around I couldn't stand.

I declined the offer and went to my next job at Kent Brushes in Bond Street, a very old, established firm that made everything from brooms to hairbrushes: they even had King George IV's toothbrush on show in the front foyer.

After several months of filing invoices, I couldn't wait to get back to nursing, so I joined a private agency in London. I remember going for my interview in my best clothes, wearing little white gloves. They were impressed. Was it the gloves that got me the job, or the fact that they loved Australian nurses in England?

I nursed some delightful, interesting patients. One was the mother of Hugh 'Binkie' Beaumont, a theatre agent who'd brought many fantastic shows to London, such as *My Fair Lady*. We sat up half the night while she told me of the antics of the film stars at parties in her son's apartment; Kay Kendall and Rex Harrison were there one night, and Kay jumped over the lounge, much to my patient's amusement.

The film star Broderick Crawford was another patient whom I looked after in the London Clinic; and there was a Lady Solomon, from the Bahamas, but she wasn't ill—she wanted a slave to pick up her clothes as she dropped them on the floor all the way down the corridor to her bedroom. I rang the agency the next day and horrified them when I said I refused to go back.

I also nursed a Jewish lady who lived at Marble Arch near Hyde Park. She wasn't ill either, but she just wanted company at night in case she had an asthma attack. I was told to make myself comfortable in a large lounge chair with footstool; pillows and blankets positioned near the end of her double bed.

'Are you sure you are quite comfortable, Sister?' she would ask several times during the night, after we'd chatted for an hour or so before sleep.

I learnt a little about Jewish culture from her. She would light the seven candles on the menorah every Friday after her family arrived. It had to be as the sun set, and then they would pray. Her kitchen was divided into halves, meat and dairy, each with its own fridge, sink and utensils. I was told not to use a meat tea towel on dairy utensils and vice versa.

She offered to take me on a trip to America as her nurse if I stayed with her all that year. But I was off on a jaunt to Scandinavia with Smiddy. I was sent back to nurse the Jewish woman later in the year. Once again she talked of going for a trip to America and wanting a nurse to go with her, implying that I could be the chosen one if I didn't leave to see my brother in Canada. But I was ready to go, and on my own.

I left London for Canada with ten pounds in my pocket. Everything was prepaid except for food between New York and Toronto. I travelled to New York on the *Carinthia*, another Cunard liner. It was the first time I'd travelled by myself, and I had a wonderful time. But funds were definitely getting low, so I pinched some bread and cheese from the dining room before disembarking.

The *Carinthia*'s engineer, who had been quite attentive on the voyage, asked if he could show me New York. Well, what could I say? I couldn't disappoint him. He took me to the United

Nations Headquarters, the Rockefeller Center and the Empire State Building. I adored New York. And it was all very 'proper'.

I only had one night there as the next I was on a train heading towards my brother, Tim. I dropped in to Niagara Falls for a night before continuing to Toronto where I caught the Canadian Pacific through the Rockies to Vancouver. Thank goodness I'd paid for food tickets to cover the three- to four-day trip. I arrived penniless to stay for six weeks with Tim and meet his future wife, Faye Drewes, an Australian from Newcastle who was working as a secretary.

Although I was booked to return on SS *Lakemba*, Tim wanted me to stay and work in Canada. I just wanted to get home to see Colin. Sometimes I've wondered what would have happened had I stayed. I may have met some charming Canadian and lived most of my life in his country, missing out on my fabulous life in the Outback.

4

Our farewell party

Mr Alan Perry spent the hour of my interview telling me what a wonderful time I was going to have at Wave Hill. He offered me the job on the condition that the general manager, Mr Peter Morris, hadn't found a nursing sister in Darwin while on a trip there. Mr Perry would ring me that night to confirm. That suited me. I kept my fingers crossed that the general manager would have found someone.

That evening, in a cab on the way to our farewell party at Smiddy's home in Point Piper, I told Wylva of my interview and the expected phone call.

'That's great, Thea. I do hope you get the job.'

'But I don't want to leave Sydney!'

'It sounds like an experience not to be missed. You take it, and if you don't like it you can always leave.'

'Yes, I guess so.'

On arrival at the party, Wylva announced that I was expecting a call about a job on a cattle station in the Northern Territory.

Everyone was so excited for me, but all I felt was trepidation. About 8 p.m., Mrs Smidlin came into the lounge where we were all watching slides of the Northern Territory.

'There's a call for you, Thea,' she said.

Apprehensive, I slowly walked to the phone. 'Hello, this is Thea.'

'Congratulations, you've got the job!' Mr Perry answered.

Oh my God, I thought, *what have I agreed to? Am I mad?* There was so much to think about. But it was hard to be miserable, with all my friends being so happy for me. I kept telling myself, *Thea, if you don't like it, you can just* leave.

5

A disorganised organised tour

There was an air of excitement as Wylva and I arrived at the CSIRO building in our taxi. Ten schoolteachers were chatting merrily to Steve and Adam, the CSIRO lecturers who were being paid to drive the twelve of us in their holiday time.

Their minibuses were rather dilapidated: one was an Austin and the other a Volkswagen. I boarded the latter with Wylva and four other schoolteachers. I was feeling sad about leaving the city, and fearful at what I'd accepted, but I decided I'd worry about that when I got to Alice in two weeks' time. This was another adventure, I told myself, which I was going to enjoy.

We passed Central Railway and Marcus Clark's department store on the right, continuing on until we turned into Parramatta Road. Just outside Sydney University, we slowed. The motor was making unusual noises—and we broke down. Unbelievable! There were, of course, no mobile phones, but we'd passed a garage not far back. Adam walked back to get help. After some band-aiding, we were off again with a new motor on order.

Somehow we managed to get to Albury, 550 kilometres from Sydney, where we were to be held up for two days while the motor was installed. This meant our minibus would not go to Adelaide where my eldest brother, Tony, now a trainee Passionist father, lived in a monastery. Fortunately I was able to join the Austin crowd for that trip, while the Volkswagen group would have to go through Broken Hill. We planned to meet up again in Port Augusta.

When I saw Tony at the monastery, he was quite shocked when I told him where I was going to work. Then he started thinking in terms of me converting the Aboriginal residents to Catholicism. Subsequently, he thought it was a good idea. I thought, but didn't tell Tony, that I wouldn't be doing any converting. He would have to do that himself.

After leaving Adelaide, we headed for Port Augusta to meet up with the VW crowd, and on the way we stayed overnight in Wilmington. The manager of our motel organised his barman to take a few of us out to see Alligator Gorge. Here we viewed the amazing Flinders Ranges. This huge mountain range was created more than five hundred million years ago, when movement of the Earth's plates caused the land to rupture and uplift. Now, erosion has reduced the range considerably. Yellow-footed rock wallabies abounded with other Australian wildlife through this beautiful landscape.

At Port Augusta we caught up to the VW and I changed vehicles again. The country to the north looked desolate but it did have the Flinders Ranges as a backdrop. From the Ranges we headed towards the smaller southern part of Lake Eyre, which is both the largest salt lake and the lowest point below sea level in Australia. It was such a different landscape, looking across the waterless lake. It was seemingly lifeless and shimmered away into the distance.

Continuing on, we discovered that the road had turned to a dirt track with either a turn-off with no sign at all, or a Y-junction with a sign pointing to nowhere in particular. Out came the compasses.

It was primitive camping with only half the cooking utensils and half the number of tents needed for the fourteen of us. We made do with sleeping on blow-up mattresses under the stars, not worrying about the tents at all. For those in the Austin without dust-proofing and air-conditioning, the trip along the dirt roads was a nightmare. They had to wear scarves over their mouths, chew gum, which helped in the production of saliva, and put Vicks up their nostrils to stop breathing in the dust.

The dust varied in colour from khaki to bright red. What a terrible sight it was to see the group sitting in their Austin with only their eyes showing, while we looked like advertisements for cleanliness in our air-conditioned VW.

But the minibuses very rarely stayed together, especially after the sun went down. This was mainly because our driver, Adam, who was doing his thesis on kangaroos, would position the spotlights on every kangaroo he saw. He would stop and, with the lights still on the kangaroo, give us a lesson on its anatomy and physiology. By the time he was finished the other bus would be miles ahead, so it was always late by the time we found their campsite, set up and cooked a meal.

We saw Woomera, where the atomic bomb tests were carried out in the 1950s and '60s. We even camped in a deserted house in the Woomera area, as the other bus was so far ahead and it was getting late. We had four walls but no roof, and we made a lovely fire in the fireplace. Here we cooked steak and eggs and had billy tea. The following morning we realised we were in a prohibited area: possibly radioactive. We didn't linger over breakfast.

After Lake Eyre we travelled for days through the Gibber Plains, flat areas covered in loose stones called 'gibbers' (from an Aboriginal word), and then on to Coober Pedy, and to the turn-off for Ayres Rock. The country was awfully dry and there was nothing as far as the eye could see but flat, treeless plains, covered with gibbers from thumbnail size to that of a man's hand.

Coober Pedy was amazing, partly because everything was underground except for two shops that between them sold everything you could imagine. One old opal miner took us down into his house. It was very comfortable but a little grubby. Wylva went six metres down a narrow mineshaft—I wasn't game.

We passed through the town of Kingoonya, which had about five buildings—really just shacks. I didn't even see Kulgera just over the border; we were past it before I noticed. But we all noticed the emus and kangaroos, wedge-tailed eagles and frill-necked lizards; we studied the stars and moon through binoculars; and we had our first wash for three days in a tank at

Marlo Bore. At Wantapella Well we watched a drunken manager try to organise the branding of his cattle.

The turn-off to Ayres Rock is about 206 kilometres south of Alice and 247 kilometres from the Rock itself. Just before the turn-off, we hit some bad luck. Our motor was running on three cylinders, and we had three flat tyres that we had to keep pumping up at twenty-five pumps each. We had no hope of getting to Ayres Rock and would have to go straight to Alice Springs.

When we were halfway into Alice, what should come chugging towards us but the Austin? The other group had been to Alice, dumped their luggage, somehow got partially dust-proofed, and were now off to Ayres Rock. So, yours truly went with them, sitting on the engine box.

We passed Curtin Springs eighty-two kilometres from the Rock, and there I observed my first Aboriginal person. My heart sank at the man's dishevelled appearance; he was filthy, with matted hair. I wondered if the Aboriginal people on Wave Hill would be in such a state.

The road to Ayres Rock was full of bulldust: a powdery, churned-up dust that lay feet deep. We very smugly passed a Pioneer tour bus completely bogged in at least two feet of bulldust. Not long after, our axles were suddenly imbedded deep in it as well. Panic! *What do we do?* Our trusty driver instructed us to collect bushes to put under and around the tyres, and after much pushing and pulling we finally got out. We continued towards the Rock—or Uluru as it is now officially called—and camped for the night.

We were up at sunrise to see Ayres Rock, which turned completely red as the sun appeared—a fantastic sight. The weather was cool and the wind unruly. It was too dangerous to climb, so we set out to explore the base of the enormous rock. As we wandered part of the way around, we discovered caves with walls covered in Aboriginal art. We were awestruck with the realisation of the thousands of years that they had been there and the thought of the people who had painted these incredible images.

6

Alice Springs to Wave Hill

For three days we explored Alice Springs and the surrounding colourful landscape: Kings Canyon, Standley Chasm, Simpsons Gap and the dry Todd River. In my eyes, the whole MacDonnell Ranges consisted of thousands of Albert Namatjira scenes, as though the artist himself had recreated them with hues of brick-red, purple, mauve and every shade of green.

Then it was time for me to start facing the music. Feeling sick in the stomach, I went to the Bank of New South Wales, as directed by Mr Perry, and picked up the letter confirming my appointment as sister/housekeeper at Wave Hill Station. Also enclosed was an introductory letter to the manager, Mr Tom Fisher.

Oh dear God, what was I doing?

I contacted Connellan Airways, an airline headquartered in Alice Springs, and confirmed the time of departure of the mail plane to Wave Hill. It was a great relief to find that the plane was delayed for one day. Of course, the following day it was time to go, and I had no excuses.

Wylva escorted me to the airport, giving me words of encouragement. 'Thea, it's going to be fabulous. I'm sure you'll love it when you get there.'

I tried putting on a brave face. We hugged farewell, then I walked to the plane, waving goodbye. As I stepped up into the Cessna, the English pilot introduced himself and offered me the co-pilot's seat. I was the only passenger amid heaps of mailbags, large boxes and engine parts.

We landed at Connellan's property, Narwietooma, where the pilot and I were given breakfast and met some most hospitable people including Edward 'Eddie' Connellan, the aviation pioneer who started the airline in 1939.

From there, it was on to Yuendumu Aboriginal Mission to pick up two passengers. As I saw all the Aboriginal people sitting or standing around, I was amazed at the blackness of their skin. Next stop, over miles of desert, was Hooker Creek, another Aboriginal settlement. The Vesteys had once run this property, but when the grazing lease expired in 1945, the government turned Hooker Creek into an Aboriginal reserve. We had lunch at the settlement manager's house, with hundreds of Aboriginal residents milling around the airstrip, watching us as we flew out.

The country changed dramatically after Hooker Creek. Gone were the vast expanses of reddish desert, sprinkled with green spinifex. Now it was timbered country, with soft green grass on undulating hills. We flew over spectacular gorges, stony creeks and the sparkling waters of the Victoria River, which wound its way through the landscape.

On approaching Wave Hill, the pilot flew around the homestead several times so I could take photos. I saw dozens of white-painted buildings with patches of green lawn and splashes of colour from the gardens. The buildings surrounded an enormous flat open area. Cattle yards were visible on the outskirts of the station. A little further on I saw a dozen or so small corrugated houses with humpies scattered around where the Wave Hill Station Aboriginals lived.

There was movement at the station as we flew over. A vehicle headed in our direction.

'That'll be Tom Fisher, coming to pick you up,' the pilot informed me.

We landed and taxied up to a fuel-storage shed on the side of the airstrip, which provided valuable shade. Opening the door, the pilot stepped out to unload the Wave Hill mailbags. It was after midday and as I exited the aircraft I felt a blast of dry, excessively hot air. The realisation hit me that I was now hundreds of miles north of the Tropic of Capricorn.

I could see dust rising as Tom's vehicle came closer, and felt the butterflies in my stomach. What would I find in this remote part of the world? Here I was about to meet my new boss and start a new job, both of which I knew very little about: just that Tom was an old hand and had recently divorced from his second wife, and that my duties would include working as his housekeeper and hostess, as well as nursing. I hoped we would get on.

The Land Rover pulled up. Tom, who was in the driver's seat, raised his hat in greeting. I saw a jovial, bald-headed, middle-aged man, and as he got out of the vehicle I observed that he was short and with a rather round stature. He shook my hand with a good firm grip. I was quite impressed. So this was Tom Fisher, the manager of Wave Hill Station.

In the back of the Land Rover was Brisbane Sambo—Tom's 'car boy', as they were called at the time—an Aboriginal man who was well into his sixties. He gave me a beautiful big smile. Brisbane had been with Tom for years, and his main job was to travel everywhere in the 4WD with his boss. He would open gates, change punctured tyres, wash the car, change the oil, and was also Tom's right-hand man to do odd jobs and run messages.

Tom picked up the mailbags and a few spare parts for various machines. We said goodbye to the pilot and drove towards the station. We chatted about my trip and Tom's life in the Northern Territory. He had come from Kyogle in New South Wales to manage the Vestey's Willeroo Station, which was on the road from Wave Hill to Katherine. During the war years he managed Manbulloo Station near Katherine, before being transferred to Wave Hill about twelve years before I arrived there. Although I knew he'd been married twice, I didn't venture my comments in that direction.

The station homestead was about thirteen kilometres from the airstrip, and I found out that we were driving on the Buchanan Highway, which runs right through the middle of Wave Hill Station and on to Western Australia. The highway was named after the first owner of Wave Hill, Nathaniel 'Nat' Buchanan, who was among the ranks of other Australian pioneer pastoralists, drovers and explorers, such as John Costello, Patrick Durack and Will Landsborough.

The whole of Wave Hill was the traditional land of the Gurindji people, who'd learnt to work alongside the new white settlers. But in 1899 there was unrest: Aboriginal people attacked the manager and his stockmen, and the original homestead on the banks of the Victoria River was burnt down in 1900.

In 1924, a heavy flood wreaked havoc on the rebuilt homestead, washing away buildings, stock and equipment worth thousands of pounds, and taking everything in its path except the flour stack. When I first visited the original Wave Hill Station several months after my arrival, all that remained was a small graveyard with weathered, unmarked stones—a rather sad, desolate place.

The present homestead, its Aboriginal name 'Jinparrak', was built about sixty-four kilometres from the Victoria River in 1924.

7

'Jinparrak'

On arrival at the homestead, the first thing I saw was the ant-bed tennis court and the lawns with wide canvas awnings stretching out from shady verandahs. This was the visitors' quarters, Tom's quarters and the smoko verandah.

'Have you had lunch, Sister?' Tom asked after we arrived.

'Yes, thank you, at Hooker Creek. They all send their regards.'

'Well, come this way and I'll show you your room.'

Tom led me through the smoko verandah, the hub of the station, a spacious area with cement and paving-stone floors. The walls on one side were made of paperbark, while the roof was covered with a thick, coarse, yellowish-grey thatch, which I found out was spinifex, the low-growing plant that thrives in the desert and holds the fragile soil together with its roots. Two lines of heavy black plastic chairs laced in yellow plastic strips faced each other with small tables scattered between. A larger table covered with a freshly ironed cloth and set with cups and saucers was in the centre of the area.

Passing the visitors' bathroom, I glimpsed a woodchip water heater for an old enamel bath. Then came a lattice room-divider, followed by a couple of visitors' rooms. At the end of the building was the radio room.

Tom informed me that the mechanic's wife, Nancy, who was also the postmistress, sent and received telegrams via radio. The Country Women's Association would have their meetings on the radio, and there was also the Galah Session, an hour of chitchat between folk on the different properties. This, according to Tom, was not to be encouraged! Our call sign on the two-way radio was 8OG, Eight Oscar Golf.

The radio room was also where I was to send urgent medical reports to the Aerial Medical Service in Darwin. This service had commenced in 1946, for the Top End only. The Royal Flying Doctor Service, based in Alice Springs, looked after the rest of the Territory. They worked in conjunction with each other, and with the WA Flying Doctor Service, based in Wyndham.

Two steps down from the verandah and a few metres from the homestead was a small corrugated-iron building. This was to be my quarters; my donga. Inside it was quite comfortable, with a single iron bed draped in a floral quilt, a timber dressing table and a mauve-painted wardrobe. There was certainly plenty of ventilation, with three doors and one window. I also had my own little shower recess just outside one of the doors, with galvanised walls and a curtain uniquely made from strips of truck tyres! On the shower-recess floor was a three-legged stool made by one of the jackaroos for the previous sister; one could use it as a footstool, or for somewhere to sit and ponder the sky, as this was the ceiling.

Fifty yards in the distance, down on the flat, was the 'thunderbox'. One only looked into it once as the pit, terrifyingly, seemed to go on forever.

'Smoko'll be at three o'clock on the verandah,' Tom said, as he carried my suitcases into my room. 'When you hear the bell, come out and meet everyone. We're ruled by bells here—one bell half an hour before a meal, so people can get ready, and the second bell for the meal.'

Tom departed with a smile and left me to contemplate my new home.

An hour later, after I'd finished unpacking, I heard the bell and, a little later, male chatter coming from the smoko verandah. Feeling uneasy, I plucked up my courage and wandered out to the grating sound of a dozen chairs scraping on the cement floor, as the predominantly male gathering stood to attention on my entry. They all turned their heads, fifteen of them, to gaze at me. To this day I remember their bright shining eyes, especially those of Jack Niven, the storekeeper, whose blue eyes twinkled the most. I should have felt nervous but they were such a friendly-looking lot.

Tom walked in, followed by a tall, confident-seeming guy. 'Aha,' said Tom, 'so you've come to join us, Sister.'

One by one I was introduced to many of the Wave Hill staff, starting with the only married woman present, Nancy Walton, the round and jovial postmistress. The confident man,

Ces Farrow, was next; he was the bookkeeper, and I would meet his wife, Lauris, and their baby son, Roger, later. Then there was Tony Clark, the tall, good-looking head stockman, and Ralph Hayes, the improvement overseer, who was lean, wiry and also quite handsome, but he looked very serious when he stared at me intently. I could feel myself blushing.

As I moved on, I felt myself relax. I met Ralph's brother, Maitlynn 'Lynn' Hayes, who had a cheeky look on his face. Garry Smith, a senior stockman, was big and strong, and I soon found out that he'd been keen on the previous sister.

The jackaroos were young, shy and delightful to meet: Pat Duggan, smiling broadly, a full-of-fun Irishman; Gunner Isberg, tanned and blond, with a cute smile, from Sweden; and Tom Joyce, an English jackaroo with thick-rimmed glasses, who looked as though he would be better suited to an office. Then the Aussies: Len Brodie, bookkeeper turned stockman; Jim Tough, from Queensland; and Rod Russell from New South Wales—all very pleasant types.

Last but far from least was Sabu Singh, with a brilliant smile on his handsome black face. Sabu, at the age of four, had been adopted by Tom at Manbulloo when he was managing there. Apparently Tom had seen Sabu's mother in the camp with her half-Indian, half-Aboriginal baby, and jokingly said, 'You better give me that piccaninny.' The next day Tom had found the baby on his doorstep. His name had been Mele, but Tom called him Sabu and it stuck.

Nancy acted as hostess, offering me a cup of tea from the hefty cast-iron pot and welcoming me to the station. 'Lauris and I are very pleased to have another white woman to support our ranks amid all these men,' she said warmly.

After smoko, Tom said, 'You should meet Emilie, your house girl, who'll clean your room and do the washing and ironing.'

We could hear some tittering just outside the verandah, where the Aboriginal 'dining-room girls' were waiting to take the crockery away. They also wanted to catch a glimpse of 'dat new sistah', so Tom called out to invite them in.

Four Aboriginal women walked in: Emilie, 'Mad' Maria, Connie and Alice. They were all in colourful cotton dresses, had bare feet and very clean, combed hair, and could not stop giggling until Tom called out, '*Karjinga*, cut it out, you fella.' *Karjinga* is a Gurindji expletive that Tom was fond of using.

Emilie was quite plump, with a wide, cheerful smile and twinkling eyes. At first glance she reminded me of Scarlett O'Hara's Mama in the movie *Gone with the Wind*. Pansy looked after the smoko and radio areas. Marian and Mad Maria were in charge of the jackaroos' and men's quarters; Alice looked after Tom's quarters; Vera, Polly and Linda were the regular dining-room girls; Ida ran the soup kitchen; Topsy helped me in the hospital; and Connie, Elsie and Barbara helped in the main kitchen, Hilda and Cushion in the laundry. They were often moved around, depending on who was pregnant or on walkabout.

Later that afternoon I was taken over to the main kitchen where the rest of the white male staff—known as the 'old men'—ate. 'Old men' were white and half-caste workers other than jackaroos and stockmen: the boundary riders, saddlers

The Aboriginal women at Wave Hill would bring their babies to Thea for a health check. She weighed the babies at the store every month.

Thea with one of her young Aboriginal patients outside the clinic.

Thea with the mail at Wave Hill.

Giving Jimmy, one of the stockmen, an injection.

Our wedding in the smoko area at Wave Hill.

Ralph and I about to leave for our honeymoon.

The Wave Hill crew
about to leave for
Thea's and Ralph's
engagement party
at Limbunya, 1961.

Ralph and I outside
our first home.

Our third home
on Wave Hill, just
completed with
men's quarters on the
left. It looked much
better with lawns
and shrubs when the
Governor General
came to stay.

A stock camp buggy loaded up with supplies. (Photo courtesy of Gunna Isberg)

Gunna and Aboriginal stockmen at work. (Photo courtesy of Gunna Isberg)

Mustering the cattle at Wave Hill.

The *Kookaburra* went missing while searching for Sir Charles Kingsford Smith's and Charles Ulm's *Southern Cross*.

Ralph and Jim Tough holding up one of the planes sent out to search for the *Kookaburra*. It met a fiery end. Part of its frame was used to make a beef cart.

Dick Smith came to Wave Hill to search for the *Kookaburra*. He's pictured here front left with, from left to right, (front) Ralph, Dick Jansen and the rest of Dick's crew.

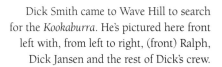

Vincent Lingiari and Ralph's Humber, 1963.

Vincent on a bronco horse, 1964.

Rounding up the children for the first day of school, 1961.

Wodular, Terrie Jones, Anthony and Linda at Gordon Downs, 1963.

David with Wodular and Sarah on the lawn at Gordon Downs, 1964.

The Christmas Day cricket match complete with goats in the outfield, 1960.

and bore mechanics. There was Harry Huddleston, the saddler, a perfect gentleman; Colin Wardell, the fencer; Alec Morton, the butcher/baker; and the cook and grader driver, Tommy 'Swannie' Swan. Their table was always set with a plastic cloth and a jar of bright-red, home-grown chillies marinating in brown vinegar. One day Swannie offered me a chilli, which I'd never tasted before. My reaction had the men in fits of laughter as I tried to wash out my burning mouth.

Next stop was the store. It contained the groceries: bags of flour, potatoes and pumpkins; clothing for the Aboriginal women and children; stockmen's clothes—practically any-thing you can think of from the early 1960s was in that store. An order was sent to Sydney every six months and the goods arrived by truck.

Across from the store was the compound for fencing and building materials. Next were the jackaroos' quarters, consisting of six rooms in a row, with a verandah on both sides. The rooms had no windows but four doors each, making them well ventilated. There was a recreation room at one end and a shower room at the other.

On the opposite side of the large flat courtyard was the main kitchen, the servery for the Aboriginal workers, the bakehouse, the meat house and the saddlers' shop, and further down were the men's quarters, followed by storage sheds for buggies, saddlery and stock-camp gear.

At the northern end of the station area was the post office cottage, where Nancy and Bill Walton lived. Fifty yards away, another corrugated-iron cottage was occupied by the bookkeeper, Ces, and his wife and baby. Each family had an Aboriginal house girl to help with the cleaning and laundry. And fifty yards further west was a second set of men's quarters.

Between the cottages and the jackaroos' quarters was the wood heap, with Chisel in charge: a very sweet, very large Aboriginal man who was completely dedicated to his vital job of fuelling the station's stoves and wood heaters.

I was amazed by the organisation of the station. Everyone, white and Aboriginal, had their jobs and seemed to do them so enthusiastically. And there was great respect from one to another, black to white and white to black.

Dinner was at six-thirty. Tom had told me to come to the smoko area when the bell rang, which I did, and we all went into the dining room together. Everyone dressed for dinner, which meant long-sleeved shirts, long trousers and ties for the men. Tom sat at the head of a very long table. I learnt that I should sit to his right and the overseer to his left, followed by any visitors to the property and then the boys according to seniority.

In the corner of the dining room was the carving table, where Pansy, Linda or Polly would place the food they'd kept warm in the pantry stove. Tom would carve the beef, asking everyone in turn, 'Roast or corn?' Tom and I would ladle the food onto the plates and the dining-room girls, dressed in a uniform of cotton aprons and matching caps, would collect the plates, serve each person to the right and take away from the left.

After dinner, coffee and tea were served on the smoko verandah, and then everyone would wander off to their rooms to read, write letters or sleep. When there were visitors, we would stay a bit later, chatting and having supper—which, I discovered later, I was also responsible for! The lighting plant was turned off at ten o'clock, so no one stayed up very late.

On that first night I lay in bed thinking about how negatively I'd felt about coming to an Outback station. I'd been expecting conditions like the early pioneers had experienced: raw timber houses with bough sheds and dirt floors. How wrong I'd been. Life here was extremely civilised, and maybe quite exciting— well, except for the pit toilet!

No, I'm not leaving yet, I thought to myself. *I can't wait to see more of this fascinating station.*

8

My first day

Early the next morning, six-thirty to be precise, Emilie appeared at my door.

'Sistah,' she said, 'cuppa tea?'

I was amazed to learn that every morning, half an hour before breakfast, when the first bell rang, each staff member was brought a cup of tea by the house girls. At 7 a.m., when the second bell rang, everyone would meet on the smoko verandah to wait for Tom. As he arrived, all stood and followed him into the dining room in order of seniority: the sister first, followed by the overseer, the stockmen and the jackaroos.

My first breakfast at Wave Hill was steak, eggs, toast, tinned butter and jam. As dinner had been, it was cooked by Swannie the relieving station cook and then carried to the pantry by the dining-room girls, who would put the hot food into the stove to keep it warm until everyone sat down. The food was then carried to the serving table.

After breakfast it was time to see my clinic. Tom escorted me past the main kitchen, stepping over open drains to a galvanised iron building, about six by four metres. Instead of windows it had push-out iron shutters held open by planks of timber. There was a small sink in one corner and a bed in the other. A table and chair sat in the middle of the cement-slab floor, under which lived a million cockroaches that were only seen at night when the whole floor would be crawling with them. Thank the Lord I wasn't called out at night very often!

That first morning I had quite a number of patients, but they came to see me more out of curiosity than a need for medical assistance. The stockmen, women and children lined up outside, waiting their turn to see the new sister. The children came in droves; whenever they got too rowdy I'd wave a syringe in the air and give a bit of a cackle, and they would disappear.

During my time as nursing sister I was called on to attend to many different cases. Lacerations, centipede bites, red-back spider bites, broken limbs, colds and flu, accidental gunshot wounds, the usual children's diseases, and pre- and postnatal care. There were no diabetes or renal problems experienced by the Aboriginal residents when I was there, because they didn't have soft drinks, rarely had sweets except sugar, and had no fatty takeaways.

Medical supplies and equipment were issued by the Aerial Medical Service: dressings, bandages, suture needles, threads, cough mixtures, antiseptics and commonly used medications. Antibiotics and anti-venom were kept in a kerosene fridge on the far wall. One of the doctors who came on their regular monthly visits informed me that the anti-snake venom, if given for the wrong bite, could kill quicker than the venom itself.

I always got a sinking feeling when I was called out of normal hours, wondering what disaster I was going to find. Although I had nursed at one of the best training hospitals in the country, it was too large a place for every nurse to work in every facility. I hadn't done a stint in emergency and this worried me. I hadn't even done any suturing; luckily, the first time wasn't for too large a laceration, and afterwards I felt relief, gaining more confidence for next time. Of course, if I wasn't sure exactly what to do, I would get on the two-way radio and talk to a doctor or nurse in Darwin, and later Katherine.

When it came to my midwifery duties, I discovered that Aboriginal women didn't express their pain when they delivered their babies. If they said they were in pain I knew there was a complication. Otherwise, they would squat under a tree and push, and there the baby was. Then someone would come to me and say, 'Sistah! Dat Violet bin hab him piccaninny.' As soon as the mother was feeling up to it, usually only a few hours later, she'd come to the clinic with her baby for a check-up. I was told about one of the dining-room girls who'd waited on the table at breakfast, delivered a baby and was back to work by lunchtime.

I concluded it was best for the Aboriginal women to have their babies the way they were accustomed to. And if an expectant Aboriginal mother had a complication, she would be examined, the Aerial Medical doctor consulted, and then she would be airlifted to Darwin. Miscarriage, ectopic pregnancy and pre-eclampsia were all possible causes.

My first day

Whenever an Aboriginal baby arrived, the mother and my assistant in the clinic, Topsy, would want me to name the child, which was such an honour. The baby also received an Aboriginal name.

In the same building as the clinic was the soup kitchen, where Ida cooked for all the station children under about four years of age. Ida would get vegetables from the garden and meat from the main kitchen to make stews and soups. The Aboriginal girls and women would sit and eat on the flat dirt outside the hospital; there was no grass. The twelve or more adorable children came to the soup kitchen every morning, benefiting from the extra nutrition.

In the 1940s the mortality rate for Aboriginal children was very high. Toddlers had difficulty surviving once their mothers had another baby and began to share out the breast milk. Also, the number of Aboriginal births was very low. I remember being told that at Waterloo and Rosewood stations, very few of the Aboriginal people had children together. This was not the case at Wave Hill when I was there; there were plenty of babies born with a relatively low mortality rate.

After breakfast I would check the soup kitchen, then wander around to the jackaroos', men's and visitors' quarters to see how the housegirls were going making beds, sweeping and doing other household jobs.

Smoko was at nine in the morning and we would all gather for a cuppa and a chat. The hospital was usually open after smoko, morning and afternoon, unless one of the stock camp work groups was in and needed more supplies.

Once a month I took the mothers and babies up to the store, to weigh the little ones and chart their progress. When the doctor came each month from Darwin, we'd vaccinate with Sabin and triple antigen, and test for TB. Sometimes I had to go out to the stock camps to vaccinate those who'd missed out.

There were members of three different tribes at Wave Hill. The Gurindji were the original nomadic people of the area, while the Warlpiri were originally from Hooker Creek. The third tribe were the Mutpura. At first I found it very difficult to work out who belonged to each tribe.

Some of the men had two or three wives; one stockman had five, as he'd inherited three when his brother died. When a man became middle-aged he would take a younger wife to look after him and his first wife as they got older. Years later, Emilie told me that her husband, Algie, one of the stockmen, was going to take a young wife. I asked her if she was happy. 'No, me don't want that,' she said, but it happened anyway and they all seemed to get on well.

Every Aboriginal person belongs to a certain skin group, which has come down from common ancestors and determines who can talk to whom. These groups prevented any form of incest from occurring. Male and female cousins were forbidden even to look at one another, so sometimes I would be told, 'No, Missus, him cousin alonga me, me no look at him.' In an effort to keep track of everyone, I started keeping a skin-group record book.

The Aboriginal workers and their families lived at a camp across Five Mile Creek from the homestead. The creek was dry most of the year. The camp—built by the Vesteys according to the Pastoral Award for Aborigines—consisted of galvanised houses on stilts. They were not inhabited when I arrived, as in each one a member of an Aboriginal family had passed away, and the other members were forbidden to return. Instead they built humpies out of iron sheets, old bags and wooden planks, just as we whites, as kids, had made our cubbyhouses. These people seemed happier living as they had done for centuries in humpies rather than houses—and it was much cooler, too.

The laundry was situated about twenty metres from the back of my quarters. It had two wood-burning coppers. The sheets and pillowslips were boiled, clothes were washed in several tubs, and clothing ironed with Mrs Potts irons: heavy, steel-plated things that were placed on the stovetop to heat before and during use. In the afternoon the Aboriginal women would congregate here and play cards while they waited their turn to iron their charges' clothes.

A wonderful tradition in the Territory is to have a siesta after lunch. At Wave Hill, lunch was at twelve o'clock; siesta was until one-thirty. The women had longer, sometimes until smoko at three.

One afternoon when I was very much enjoying a siesta, I heard a great commotion coming from the laundry. It sounded as though someone was being murdered. I went to investigate. There was six-foot Hilda with a heavy Mrs Potts iron in her outstretched hand, about to bring it down on Vera's head. I raced over, grabbing Hilda's arm, only to have her glare at me and start to bring the iron down on *my* head. The other girls came to my rescue, grabbing Hilda and dragging her away. Never again would I try to intervene in a fight or argument between Aboriginal people.

The other white women on the station, Lauris and Nancy, lived in corrugated cottages on the outskirts of the complex. I only ever saw them at smoko and when everyone got together for a special occasion. Of course, Lauris was busy with her baby, Roger, but I wonder now, years later, with only three white women on the station, why we didn't get on well together. We each led our own lives. Maybe my shyness was mistaken for aloofness.

9

A Wave Hill awakening

It was Saturday night, my first weekend at Wave Hill. Tom had consented to all the stock camps coming into the station for the weekend, as often in the middle of the stock season the boys wouldn't see the homestead for up to six weeks.

After dinner we all went over to the recreation room for a staff get-together. The room had push-out windows all round, and was large enough to contain a table-tennis table, a billiard table, and several bookshelves filled with an assortment of books and magazines. Johnny Cash's 'El Paso' was on the record player; that song will always remind me of the old Wave Hill.

The boys were having a few beers, courtesy of Tom, and as I didn't like beer I probably had a soft drink. Tom asked me to dance; we moved around the room, a mountain of flesh between us. The boys seemed content just to drink. After the second dance with Tom, I noticed that the married couples had left. I, too, said goodnight.

Arriving at my donga, I put on my pyjamas and got into bed. Suddenly, the door burst open and there was Garry, one of the stockmen. He was very drunk and was demanding that he talk to me.

I was in shock. I felt quite frightened. Somehow I managed to say, 'Excuse me, I don't want to talk to you. Would you please *leave*.'

I knew that Garry had been in love with the previous sister, who'd left six weeks before I arrived. 'I have to tell you a few things,' he said. He was leaning over me, shaking his finger at me, and raving about how Tom would proposition me. Garry explained that he'd come to warn me about what had happened to the previous sister—so on and on he went!

In between his drunken babble, I kept hysterically shouting, 'If you don't get out of here, I'm going to start screaming.'

Suddenly, this totally drunken moron interrupted me and said, 'You don't have to do that. I'll scream for you!'

With that, he went outside, hollering at the top of his voice. I don't know what he was yelling because as soon as he'd departed I jumped out of bed, frantically raced to lock the three doors and collapsed on the bed in dread. I heard a commotion outside: voices raised, swearing, a scuffle, then a knock on my door.

'You all right, Sister?'

It was Tony Clark. He and Ralph Hayes had come running when they heard Garry yelling out. Tom, meanwhile, had seen Garry leave the recreation room and followed him. When he walked out of my room, Tom flattened him, so he was lying on the ground by the time Ralph and Tony arrived.

To my Knights in Shining Armour, I called out, 'I'm okay, but just go away and leave me alone.'

In retrospect, although I was terrified at the time, I think Garry was lonely, miserable and drunk, and probably wanted some female company. He'd also noticed me and Tom dancing and thought he should warn me: but there was no need, as Tom always treated me like a daughter, and I think he was protective of all young women.

I didn't sleep much that night and when morning arrived I knew I had to decide on one of two options. If I was worried about my safety I should pack my bags and leave—but I realised I didn't want to leave. Wave Hill and its people fascinated me.

Tom came around before breakfast, full of apologies. He told me that Garry was being transferred to another station. He also praised his boys, Ralph and Tony, and hoped that I would stay. He informed me that Ralph had become the new overseer.

'It was a very distressing incident,' I told him, 'but I'd still really like to stay. I've decided just to say a few words to the boys so they don't get the wrong idea about me.'

So that's what I did, at breakfast.

'Sister wants to say a few words to you boys,' announced Tom.

I stood up and all the boys stood to attention, their heads bent down. All except Tony, who stared at me. So, having no one else to look at, I directed my little talk to him. 'I just want to say how shocked I was at what happened last night. Please don't anyone presume that they can come to my room uninvited. In fact, I'm going to ask Tom for a rifle to have in my quarters, and by George I will use it if I have to.' I 'forgot' to mention that I'd never held a gun in my life.

It was a very quiet meal.

Tony was most insulted that I'd directed my reprimand to him as though he was the guilty party and not one of the heroes. He was such a joker that he never let me forget it.

10

The cracked hide and the watering hole

At Wave Hill life was different to anything I'd ever known. I felt excited and was eager to discover more about this fifteen thousand square-kilometre property with its forty-odd subartesian bores and the Victoria River running through it.

One lunchtime Tom asked me if I'd like to go for a 'run' out to one of the property's four stock camps. This was Number Three Camp, run by Lynn Hayes with Gunner, his jackeroo.

As we drove up to the camp we could see the boys, Lynn and Gunner, under the bough shed. The Aboriginal stockmen were sitting in groups, chatting or playing cards. Camp ovens and billy cans lay around the campfire, which was surrounded by a carpet of grey ash. Swags were scattered about the flat; the horses' saddles and bridles were hanging on rails. As the vehicle pulled up, the boys came out to greet us. Tom, who'd downed a few beers before we left, decided to sit under the bough shed and have a sleep.

The Vestey cattle stations were 'dry' at the time, meaning no alcohol was permitted for anyone but the manager, and that was mainly for him to share with VIP visitors. Tom seldom shouted the staff a drink. Occasionally someone's 'hide' would 'crack': they felt desperately in need of alcohol. A vehicle would sneak off to fetch a cargo of grog from the nearest 'watering hole', which in our case was the Top Springs roadhouse, 160 kilometres to the north. Staff wouldn't turn up for work and a jackaroo was usually sent down to investigate.

One time, Ralph and Sabu were ordered to find out why the saddler Colin Cerdergreen hadn't been seen in a couple of days. When they arrived at his place there was no answer. They tried pushing the door but met resistance. Colin was dead just inside. He had cut his throat.

Quite a few men came to the Territory to escape problems from their pasts. They did their work, no one bothered them, and they found peace except when there was alcohol around. Another Colin, a 'Sydneyite'—bright and intelligent—became very attached to one of the Aboriginal girls. They lived together and had three children, and the Inland Mission made them get married. Sadly, Colin died of alcoholic poisoning some years later.

Back in the stock camp, as Tom continued to snooze, I chatted with the boys.

'Do you ride, Sister?' Lynn asked.

I had always longed to become a good horsewoman, but

living in the city my opportunities to ride were rare. Three very quiet horses were all I could brag of.

'Of course I do,' I replied

'Would you like to have a ride?'

'Oh yes, Lynn, I'd love to.'

Gunner was sent off to get Codeine, the previous sister's grey stockhorse. They saddled her up and Lynn helped me get on. I gave her a bit of a kick and nothing happened. I tried again. Codeine did not move. So Lynn gave her a whack on the backside, and away we went.

Codeine had galloped about ten metres when the stirrup leather suddenly came undone and down I went, landing on my chest. It all happened so quickly.

I couldn't breathe, but I could hear. And what I heard was Lynn laughing uncontrollably, while trying to ask me, 'You all right, Sister?'

His laughter was so infectious I got the giggles myself and found it very difficult to breathe and laugh at the same time. When I got to my feet I made the boys promise they wouldn't tell Tom. I should have said, *Don't tell anyone*, because at dinner that night Lynn's brother, Ralph, asked, 'What happened to your forehead, Sister?'

I had a small abrasion above my right eye. I didn't think anyone would notice but, of course, most knew about my accident.

Looking daggers at Ralph and Lynn, I retorted, 'I ran into a door.'

The boys were trying to suppress their laughter while Tom glanced around, quite confused.

11

Bushfire

At the end of October 1960, a bushfire started about forty-eight kilometres from the station. Every man was mustered up to help put it out. I insisted on going as well, so we all went after dinner.

The fire was raging for miles, racing towards the bore country, which is the best country on the station. I'd thought I was going out to fight the fire, but instead I had to drive the jeep and follow the firefighters. Imagine me driving a jeep by myself, let alone over scrub and rocks! The old engine would give one almighty roar, and then I'd stall the damn thing. No one to help me, so I just had to get it going the best I could. I kept up with them, but I'll never know how. I was unable to see more than a few feet ahead even though it was a moonlit night—and a good thing, too, as when I saw the area in the daylight, some days later, I was shocked at what could have happened. Valuable experience, I guess.

Later on that night I finally had my 'whack' at the flames, with hessian bags and tree branches. We fought on until three-thirty in the morning, and then turned for home, as the fire had headed off into gullies and more barren country.

But by morning the wind had changed, and the fire had come back over to the bore country. It was a frightfully hot and windy day. Out everyone went again, except me: I'd had enough. Even the house girls went out to fight; they thought it wonderful until they had to start dancing around the flames in their bare feet. Everyone stayed out battling the fire all day and night, arriving back the following afternoon, absolutely exhausted.

That was a Saturday afternoon, and that night there was a party on at the Wave Hill police station, seventeen kilometres away. The firefighting didn't stop the men. We all went. Basil Courts was the policeman, and his lovely wife, Molly, was a superb cook and hostess. By the end of the evening I was pooped too, as there were about thirty men who all wanted to dance and only four women.

We danced on the cement floor in the breezeway: boogie-woogie, rock and roll. We had so much fun. I loved to dance.

One evening not long after the fire, Alice, one of the dining-room girls, came to me with her sick baby, Raymond. I asked her why she hadn't brought him up to the clinic that afternoon. 'Him gets sick quick fella, Sistah,' she replied.

Poor little Raymond was very ill. He showed signs of pneumonia. Quickly getting on to the Aerial Medical Service, I relayed the critical condition of my patient to the doctor on call. Antibiotics were ordered; permission given to use the antiquated oxygen tent Tom produced from his quarters.

Although Raymond required evacuation, medical planes back then weren't equipped to fly eight hundred kilometres and land at night, so we had to wait till the morning for his evacuation. Tom and I sat with Alice. Tom was a wonderful support; he'd seen some tragic emergencies in his years in the bush. We had an emergency situation and there was nothing we could do. We were helpless.

In the early hours of the morning, baby Raymond passed away. His mother was devastated, and so were Tom and I. I felt a terrible feeling of failure, but Tom restored my confidence with, 'You did all you possibly could.'

Alice took her baby home, and the next day he was wrapped in a blanket and buried in the graveyard on the other side of the Aboriginal camp. The funeral was terribly sad, with much weeping and wailing.

12

New responsibilities

One could presume that living on an outback station in the Northern Territory could get rather lonely or boring, but that is far from the truth. Everyone made their own fun: reading, listening to music, playing cricket, arm-wrestling and training horses for the all-important races at the Negri, of which I was about to learn more about.

I kept discovering new responsibilities such as the vegetable garden, and the lawns and flowerbeds in front of the homestead. I found plenty of packets of seeds in the store, and having had some experience as a child growing vegetables and flowers, I planted lots of everything and was surprised when it all thrived.

The vegetable garden was run by Baker Dolly, a young Aboriginal woman with blonde hair who had come in from the desert with her blond-headed children some years before. She always worked with one of her children sitting on her hip. Cracker, who helped the butcher, was also Baker Dolly's offsider in the garden.

Every imaginable vegetable could be successfully grown in the dry season. During the wet, however, only capsicum, shallots, watermelon and rockmelon flourished. Summer salads consisted of potato or rice. No one had heard of baked-vegetable salads back then, which is a pity as we had plenty of potatoes, onions and pumpkins brought in with the supply truck every six months.

You can imagine the state of the flour after six months: creeping with weevils. However, when the bread is cooked, you don't notice—it's a bit like multigrain!

I was expected to serve supper to the visitors who arrived nearly every night during the dry season. They came in by the hundreds: travellers, Vestey guests, and contractors working on the station. One month there were six hundred visitors, and Tom and I would entertain them on the smoko verandah.

The first night we had guests, I went out to the pantry to boil the kettle and found the fire in the fuel stove had gone out. The girls had gone for the day; there was no electric jug; we had 110DC power with no electrical whitegoods. Even the lights went out at ten o'clock. What to do?!

That was when Ralph came to my rescue. He lit the fire and showed me what was available for supper: Jatz biscuits, tinned cheese and gherkins. That's all we ever had. After that, whenever visitors came, Ralph helped me get supper. He was so supportive, sweet and helpful. We started to get to know each other.

There were thousands of feral donkeys on Wave Hill and Tom would occasionally take the 'weapon carrier' out to do a spot of shooting. The weapon carrier was a vehicle originally designed for desert warfare that had seats on either side of the rear open area for carrying troops. The first time I saw these feral animals was when Ralph asked one weekend if I would like to go with him, as he and the boys were going shooting, so off I went. After driving for forty kilometres, we cut across country to where the donkeys had last been seen. I was packed in with cushions—treated like royalty, thank goodness—as we bounced over bushes and thick scrub and into creek beds.

Finally we found the donkeys, which just stood staring at us while the boys popped them off one by one with rifles. It was horrible. The boys kept telling me it was necessary. 'The donkeys are feral pests,' they said. But I still wouldn't talk to them all the way home.

A couple of days later, I went with Tom and some of the boys to deliver stores to a stock camp. On the way back, the men started shooting at feral donkeys and brumbies too; these animals were there in their hundreds. Gradually I got used to the slaughter.

When I arrived in 1960, the station roads were still graded by Pompeii, an older Aboriginal man, using a fire plough that was pulled by up to forty donkeys. Pompeii would drive the donkey team with his family walking behind the plough, throwing any rocks off the new road.

As years went by we graduated to graders, and Ralph employed a driver nicknamed Claypan. Pompeii retired to the camp.

*

'How are the dairy cows going, Thea?' Jim Tough, one of the stockmen, asked at breakfast one morning.

'Beg your pardon?' I replied.

'The sister is in charge of the milkers and the milking team,' Jim said, a cheeky look on his face. Everyone around the table started smirking at my discomfort.

So after breakfast I walked up to the dairy, which was halfway between the homestead and the Aboriginal camp. There, two older Aboriginal men, Jacko and Jerry, were busy milking two Shorthorn cows. Two other cows stood waiting in the old yard. The calves were making quite a racket as they'd been locked up since the night before.

'Is everything going okay, Jerry?' I asked.

'Yes, Missus, him good milker this one.' He pointed to the cow he was milking.

Knowing absolutely nothing about dairy cows, I quite happily left them to it and went on my rounds, via the kitchen, to find out what happened to the three buckets of milk that were delivered every day. One went to the soup kitchen for the children, and the other two to the main kitchen.

The cows weren't the only animals that I supervised: orphaned foals were brought in from the camp for me to look after. I would feed them powdered milk when I fed the toddlers each day. Once I watched the breaking in of a few wild horses. I thought Frank Frith, the Aboriginal horse breaker, was going to get his skull kicked in. One poor stallion ripped his flank open; the tear was about a foot in length. I brought needles, thread, Dettol and rags. It took six boys to hold the stallion down. I couldn't get through his tough hide, so I became the instrument nurse and Ralph did the sewing up. The wound eventually healed with regular powdering of sulphur to dry it out and stop infection. I called him Hyperion, one of the twelve Titans of Greek mythology.

13

Initiation

One October the temperature had risen to around thirty-eight degrees Celsius and continued to rise unmercifully. No rain came to relieve the unbearable heat, and we had no fans or air-conditioning. In the Territory they call it the suicide month.

One was continually running to the hessian waterbags found hanging on the verandahs, with an enamel mug suspended on a wire hook waiting to be used by all and sundry. It was too hot to eat, too hot to sleep. If one wanted to lose weight, it was an ideal environment. I'd resorted to sleeping on a stretcher outside, as the past couple of nights panting in the heat and brushing off spiders and moths were more than I could bear.

Peter Morris, the Vestey general manager, was arriving with Reginald Durack, the company's pastoral inspector, for a few days of routine inspection. Mr Durack was in charge of overseeing all the company managers in the area; he was also a cousin of the well-known pioneering Durack family from Argyle Station (which is now under Lake Argyle). The men arrived in a Beechcraft Baron aeroplane, owned by the Vesteys, which Mr Morris flew whenever he came to Darwin. The staff of Wave Hill were in a frenzy—you would have thought royalty was visiting!

It was my first meeting with Peter Morris, as he'd been in the Northern Territory when I had my job interview in Sydney. He was a good-looking man backed up by a bucketload of charm. Make no mistake, though: behind the charisma was an astute man who knew a lot about people and never failed to pinpoint their strengths and weaknesses. Everyone called him Mr Morris.

Several days later, Tom had to go with Messrs Morris and Durack to inspect a property north of Wave Hill called Tipperary, which was for sale. This meant that Ralph was in charge for two weeks while Tom was away.

Ralph had always been a cattleman of the north. He'd grown up on Waterloo and Rosewood stations, which his father, Dick Hayes, and mother, Mary, had managed from 1936. The war years brought separation and divorce to Mary and Dick; and the three children, Ralph, Lynn and Milton, were scattered among relatives and friends. Ralph was sent to Tom at Manbulloo Station, where he and Sabu grew up together. The family reunited and plans were made to buy Roper Valley Station, but disaster struck: Dick was diagnosed with leukaemia and died six weeks later. This left the family penniless. Before going to Wave Hill, Ralph gained more cattle experience working with his grandfather—'Squizzy' Taylor—in the abattoirs and cattle yards of Cannon Hill, Brisbane. It should be noted that he was not the gangster Squizzy Taylor.

While Tom was away with Mr Morris, Ralph would wander down to the hospital to chat and I would pick his brains about the Aboriginals resident on the station. He knew them all; he could even speak their languages, Gurindji and Warlpiri.

They were such happy people, working on the station during the cattle season and going 'walkabout' in the wet.

After the stock camps closed each wet season, the Aboriginal employees would take it in turns to go walkabout, leaving some staff to work around the station on maintenance, fencing and looking after the bores. Walkabout usually lasted a couple of months and participants would 'go bush', living on kangaroos, emus and bush tucker. Before they left on walkabout, they were usually issued with a month's rations: a bag of flour, a pound of tea, two or three pounds of sugar, plus baking powder, a tin of golden syrup or jam, and a few sticks of tobacco; quite a load for the female walker, who usually had to be the packhorse.

It meant no bogey—as the Aboriginals called a bath—no washing hair, no looking clean for the missus.

Some of the Aboriginal people would spend their walkabout at other stations, visiting relatives, often getting a lift on a vehicle; but many would walk as they had done for centuries. They usually returned noticeably thinner.

Ces Watts, who later became the pastoral inspector for the Vesteys, told me that when he'd been at Sturt Creek in 1952, a group of Aboriginal people walked in from the desert. They had very little English and no clothes, and the women and children were terrified of white people. Those at Sturt gave them food and rations, and then they went off, out to the Tanami Desert on walkabout again.

Walkabout time was when the Aboriginal people held most of their corroborees and initiation ceremonies. But during the stock season, if there were no cattle to watch in the stock camps, you'd sometimes see Aboriginal stockmen have an impromptu corroboree, playing their didgeridoos and clacking sticks. There would be initiation ceremonies, and occasionally some of the whites would be invited to rainmaking corroborees and women's corroborees.

14

The stock camps

Whenever Ralph was heading out to the stock camps, he would invite me to go along with him. I was always thrilled and keen to see what the camps were all about.

A typical stock camp in those days consisted of about eighty horses and fourteen mules, two Aboriginal horse tailors, ten Aboriginal stockmen, a head stockman and his jackaroo. The Aboriginal workers stayed in the stock camp all their working lives, starting out as horse or bullock tailors, becoming stockmen, and then returning to horse or bullock tailoring as they became aged. The bullock tailors were older Aboriginal stockmen who had four or five young Aboriginal children with them who looked after the mob of bullocks that had been mustered. They would tail them on their horses, not far from the stock camp while the stockmen went on mustering to get more bullocks. The bullock tailors would also watch the mob at night by riding around them to quieten them. When the mob was ready, the tailors would hand them over to the drover.

The horse tailors' job before daylight was to go out on the old night horse looking for the mob of younger horses. Condamine bells were put around the necks of the mules so that the horse tailors could hear where the mob was grazing. The horses were 'hobbled': hobbles are leather straps with links and a swivel placed around a horse's fetlocks to restrict its movement. This meant the horses could move around but not wander too far away. The horse tailors had to catch the horses by their neck straps, put the bridles on, remove the hobbles and take the animals back to the camp, ready for the stockmen.

According to Tom there were seventy thousand cattle on Wave Hill and two thousand horses. There were no boundary fences, but scattered yards in different areas of the station.

The men would muster the cattle into the yards and the head stockman or the top Aboriginal stockman would ride in on a bronco. This horse would be fitted with a 'bronco saddle' that had a rope tied to a hook on its side so the stockman could lasso a beast and use his horse to haul it to the 'bronco panel', made of thick timber, where the other stockmen would pull the beast to the ground. It would then be branded, ear-tagged, castrated and de-horned as required.

Here are some details about the four stock camps on Wave.

Number One Camp—with Sabu as head stockman, his jackaroos Pat Duggan and Tom Joyce—covered the north-western area around the river country: Catfish, McDonald, Mountain Springs, Gills Creek, Wattie Creek, and Seal Gorge where there was Aboriginal art but it was *gudardji*, bad medicine, to go there.

Number Two Camp, run by Tony Clark and the jackaroo Colin Cameron, was in the river country around Hooker Creek and bordering on the neighbouring property, Inverway, which was owned by Peg and Pat Underwood, pioneers of the Territory who'd taken up their cattle station in the middle of the Vestey stations. It was called 'in the way' by the Vestey people, hence Inverway by the Underwoods. Number Two also encompassed Sambo, Gordy Springs, Number Twenty-Nine Bore, Yankee Doodle Plain, Neave Gorge and MacDonald Yard.

Lynn, Gunner and, later, Pat Duggan ran Number Three Camp. It covered the bore country, which encompassed about forty artesian bores, and the 'outstation', Cattle Creek, a very isolated little station that was part of Wave Hill on the edge of the Tanami Desert, where Joy and Jim Warren and their daughter, Mandy, looked after the stud Shorthorn bulls for use on the main station.

I was driven out to Cattle Creek a few times, enjoying time with the Warren family. Jim had his own aeroplane, an Auster: they were called 'rag and bone' planes because of their fabric covering. Jim often flew in to Wave Hill to pick up the mail. I was told that some years earlier, a gentleman had landed on the station airstrip in an Auster to refuel. When the aviation fluid was being pumped in, some static electricity caused a spark. The plane caught alight and burnt to the ground. The story went that the steel frame from the burnt plane was so strong, the men were able to make a butcher trolley for the 'killer' (a bullock slaughtered for its meat) to be carted to the kitchen. I saw the trolley there in 1960.

The stock camps

Number Four Camp was run by Jim Tough and Len Brodie. Their job was to attend to the boundaries for the handover of cattle with neighbouring properties. Mustering on unfenced boundaries required notice to be given to these stations beforehand. The stock camps from both stations would muster together, and then each station would take their rightful cattle back to their respective properties. One tried to avoid using one's own brand for a killer.

To get a killer in the stock camp, the stockmen would muster a few cattle, keeping them as quiet as possible to avoid overheating. One stockman on horseback would shoot the killer. The beast would then have its throat cut to bleed out. The hide would be removed for hobbles and straps, and then the beast would be very carefully cut into sections to be salted and hung. Everyone loved the rib bones from a fresh killer.

I learnt about the various parts of a killer. How delicious were the 'kyii' bones or floating ribs, and the 'sweetbreads', the small intestine. Lynn had a bet with me that he would somehow get me to eat 'prairie oysters', calf testicles, before next holidays. I wasn't game to eat anything at all in his camp, as much as he tempted me with all sorts of delicious-smelling food. Consequently I won the bet, and he had to take me out for dinner in Sydney when the holidays arrived.

Nearly every afternoon I went out on the 'run' with Ralph. We were getting to know each other very well and becoming the best of friends.

Someone we often caught up with, driving around the station, was Pat Bellamy, the bore mechanic. His job was crucial to the survival of the animals. He made sure all the subartesian bores were operating properly, pumping their water by windmill into tanks to keep the troughs full and the cattle watered.

While we drove around, Ralph would also check the bores that watered the hundreds of cattle. Before the wet as it got drier and drier, with very little wind, someone was needed at these bores to start their motors, so some had an Aboriginal family living on-site.

One weekend Ralph and I, with some of the boys, drove to Sambo, a delightful spot on the Victoria River. There was a gravel crossing near a tall cliff and a large waterhole with a gravel bottom, and the area was lined with paperbark and bloodwood trees. The river was about thirty metres wide at Sambo. What a beautiful river, with its many fishing and swimming sites.

The water was teeming with catfish and their nasty spikes. The other fish, including bream, were much better eating but harder to catch. I caught two catfish and a turtle—but it got away. We thought we might catch a barramundi, as they were prevalent at Inverway only twenty-three kilometres upstream, but no luck.

The further north you went, the better the barramundi. Occasionally someone would turn up at the station with a couple of these delicious fish. The cook would bake them whole in the oven and we would thoroughly enjoy this delectable change of diet.

While Ralph and I fished at Sambo, the others went hunting freshwater crocodiles that were two to three metres long. The boys said they were harmless, but no way would you get me in the water if they were close at hand. Two crocs were shot but the boys were only able to get one ashore. The Aboriginal staff had their favourite delicacy that night, barbecued crocodile. We had catfish for breakfast; they weren't bad. Anything would be a welcome change from beef, beef, beef, three times a day.

The Victoria River is about 560 kilometres long and starts at Riveren, part of Inverway Station—where Terry Underwood, Peg and Pat's daughter-in-law, wrote her book *In the Middle of Nowhere*—through to Humbert River Station, which was taken up by Charlie Schultz when he was only about nineteen. Charlie also wrote a book about his experiences, *Beyond the Big Run*, and lived there with his wife, Hessie. The river continues on through Victoria River Station and Timber Creek; Bradshaw Station, named after the fellow who found the Bradshaw rock paintings in 1891; Bullo River, where Sara Henderson wrote her book *From Strength to Strength*; and then out to sea through Queens Channel. The river lends itself to the unfolding of great stories to be passed down through the generations.

15

A big surprise

After inspecting Tipperary Station, Tom returned to Wave Hill by plane later in 1960. Peter Morris dropped him off, before continuing on to Darwin, thence to Sydney. The Vesteys did not buy Tipperary.

I wandered around to Ralph's room after spending the afternoon in the clinic. He greeted me with, 'I've told Tom I'm going to marry you.'

'You said *what*?' I replied. 'You're joking.' I knew Ralph was very keen, but I hadn't expected a proposal. I'd only been there six weeks. I was overawed and thrilled, 'cause I really liked him. But did I love him enough?

'No, I'm serious,' he replied.

I started to laugh. 'Don't I have any say in this?'

Taking me into his arms, he gently said, 'Well, will you marry me?'

'You're supposed to get down on your knees to propose,' I said, still laughing.

Looking closely at Ralph, I could see that he was serious. The look in his eyes was solemn, intent and yet very gentle. We melted together. It felt so comfortable. The heavens didn't open up and I didn't see stars, but I knew it was right. The first time Ralph had kissed me it was a friendly, non-sexy kiss. We'd shared a nice platonic kiss each night—this one was entirely different!

Over the past six weeks we'd become mates, buddies, the best of friends. I'd wondered about the possibility of romance, as I really liked Ralph, but he didn't appear to be the romantic type. Now everything changed. Here was this gorgeous romantic man with whom I'd eaten practically every meal since my arrival, gone off for jaunts to the stock camps nearly every afternoon, played table tennis and billiards in the rec room, and helped entertain hundreds of visitors. And he wanted to marry me. And it was only six weeks since we'd met!

I thought how fortunate I was to meet my future husband on the station; to be able to get to know someone so well by living in the same domain. *How difficult it must be elsewhere,* I thought, *dating once or twice a week, and hoping you've picked the right one.*

I wrote to my mother,

I'm very happy here. The overseer has fallen in love with me, and proposed already. He is terrific, but I just don't quite know what to think of everything, it's all been so sudden. We do get on wonderfully well, and feel we know one another well enough to plan for the future.

Poor Tom had nearly died of shock when Ralph told him. He was then so happy he proceeded to drink himself silly for two days. He was like a child in the way he wanted me and Ralph, and any visitors who happened to be there, to come to his quarters and listen to him babble on about nothing. I was told that this didn't happen often; a good thing, too, as no one could get any work done.

In November, not long after he proposed, Ralph was sent to Limbunya, another Vestey station, about 160 kilometres north-west of Wave. He had to relieve the manager, Ray Jansen, while he and his wife Pat and family went on their bi-yearly two-month holiday.

I thought I would be lost without my mate, but on Wave Hill we were like one big happy family. The Aboriginal people were all part of that family, a little like in the television show *Downton Abbey*: everyone had their position whether as a white or an Aboriginal employee in helping to run a big station. The Aboriginals were under the umbrella of the manager and over-seer, and the nursing sister supervised their health. In return, our quarters were cleaned, our washing done, the cattle mustered and branded. Everyone respected the role of everyone else.

While Ralph was away, I kept busy. There was always plenty to do in looking after visitors, many of whom were Vestey people travelling through on holidays.

The head stockman Tony Clark was Ralph's best friend and had been commissioned by Ralph to look out for me while he was away. Tony was a sturdy, strong friend, always there when you needed support, always interested in everything and everyone around him.

Often, in the late afternoon, we would wander over to the kitchen where someone would produce a bottle of Scotch, secretly transported via a visitor or a trip to Top Springs. I'd never tasted whisky before and with good company I really enjoyed it.

Ralph was to come over before Christmas so that we could officially announce our engagement at a party. However, the wet season started early that year, at the beginning of November, and all the rivers were overflowing, especially the Victoria. Crossing was impossible at the Wave Hill police station until New Year's, and then Gum Creek and Gills Creek were up between the police station and Limbunya. At least we had good airstrips on the stations, so we received our mail and had access to evacuation if necessary. There was no engagement party yet, but heaps of well-wishing cards arrived from down south.

16

Christmas at Wave

Christmas was fast approaching. According to Tom, the custom was that all the white staff on the station could place an order for the alcoholic beverage of their choice. A truck was then dispatched to Top Springs with a trustworthy driver. The road to Top Springs was weatherproof and the truck returned a week before Christmas, but no one was allowed to collect their order until Christmas Eve, with the exception of the boss. Two days before Christmas, Tom took his supply, drank until Christmas Eve, and then stopped just as everyone else got their grog. He became sober and virtuous, and annoyed with those who were drinking and enjoying themselves. 'Aren't they disgusting, drinking so much?' he mumbled on several occasions. If only he could have seen himself two days before.

Despite the heat, everyone dressed up for Christmas dinner. The men even wore ties, as had been the custom every night at the station until they'd complained to Tom that as I didn't always wear stockings to dinner, why should they have to wear ties? Tom had agreed, but the dress code was still long-sleeved shirts and long trousers for dinner, and ties for special occasions, such as for visiting VIPs or for a wedding.

For Christmas dinner we ate station-bred chicken and Vestey ham that was sent up from Sydney, one to each station. Christmas turned out to be the only time we got to taste ham, until several years later when we bred a few pigs and learnt to smoke cuts of pork in an old fridge with a slow fire underneath. That first Christmas Day was okay, but I think we were all remembering family Christmases. I was a little homesick, and I think some of the boys were too.

On New Year's Eve all of us were invited to the Wave Hill police station, where we'd attended the post-bushfire party a couple of months earlier. The police station was in the Wave Hill settlement, located on a small rise on the opposite side of the Victoria River.

I'd learnt a bit more about the settlement since I'd last visited. It was a small township built for the Warlpiri tribe, who'd been sent there by the federal government from Hooker Creek. Perhaps there were believed to be too many Aboriginal people at Hooker Creek—I'm not sure. We had a few Warlpiri employees at Wave Hill. They didn't seem to get on well with the Gurindji staff, or so I heard, as they were considered outsiders in the Gurindji territory.

The settlement consisted of a manager's house, storehouse, schoolhouse and teacher's house, and quite a few timber cottages built for the Aboriginal families. These suburban-type houses had stoves, washing machines, fridges, freezers and furniture.

The residents preferred to sit outside on the ground most of the time and to cook on a campfire; when they ran out of firewood, they'd chop up the furniture. Confusion reigned as to what the washing machine and the fridges were for. No one taught the residents how to use these appliances; money was poured in for material amenities and that was it. According to the settlement manager's wife, a freshly caught crocodile was found in one washing machine and dirty clothes in the freezer. Christmas 1960 saw education for Wave Hill's Aboriginal children just around the corner with the arrival of a teacher, Jill Booth, and her husband, Ian, handyman and bus driver. From the start of the school year the children were to be picked up every morning by Ian and taken to the settlement schoolhouse.

On our arrival at the settlement and police station on New Year's Eve, about twenty of us were greeted warmly by Molly and Basil Courts. We were summoned to the lower area of the two-story house where two breezeways crossed in the middle to form four gauzed rooms.

To get the show on the road, Molly and Basil had organised a party game. I was told to sit in a particular chair while someone was blindfolded and turned around three times. Next, they had to try and find me and, if they did, they could kiss me. *Yuck!* I thought, but I wasn't going to be a piker and spoil everyone's fun.

Everyone knew that Tom Joyce, the English jackaroo with glasses who looked more suited to an office than a stock camp, was a little infatuated with me; no one missed anything in our small community. Consequently, he was the chosen one. As soon as the blindfold went on, Frank Frith—the large, jovial

Aboriginal horse breaker—replaced me in the chair. Everyone was trying not to laugh as Tom Joyce completed his three turns, giddily and eagerly reaching out to grab me. He planted a big smoochy kiss on Frank's lips! The crowd roared. Tom ripped off his blindfold and shrank in embarrassment, but not for long as we all gave him loud applause for being such a good scout.

Dinner was superb. We weren't used to such tasty food at the station. The pièce de résistance was the dessert: bombe alaska with homemade ice-cream, covered in meringue, placed on a tray, doused with brandy, ignited, and brought to the table as a flaming mountain of luscious, creamy meringue.

At the time very fire-conscious, Frank jumped up to put it out with his hat. There were cries from the crowd, 'Sit down, you stupid bastard!'

It tasted fabulous. It amazed me that anyone would even think of creating something so exotic in such unbearable heat.

The next day we all played cricket on the flat outside the police station: Team Cattle Station versus Team Police Station & Settlement. We had a very enjoyable and happy day, with young kid goats running through the cricketers.

During the wet season when the stock camps were closed down, everyone was employed doing maintenance in and around the station. I had a chance to really get to know the men and hear their stories about Wave Hill and its characters. Here's one story Tony Clark told me, which happened before I arrived.

Peter Morris had been over to France to purchase a Percheron stallion to increase the size of his wagonette and bronco horses.

He'd also bought, in Australia, two thoroughbred colts—one by Wayside Inn and the other by Newtown Wonder, two very well-known thoroughbred stallions. His three new horses arrived at Wave Hill together.

Mr Morris was flying around the Territory and intended to call in to look at his horses, so that morning Tom Fisher sent Jim Tough and Tony Clark down to repair and paint the stables, where Treve, the jet-black Percheron, was housed.

Jim was painting the stables and yards white. (The company only ever provided two lots of paint, white or red!) Treve was in the yard where Jim was working, and the stallion kept poking his big head in the path of Jim's brush, until Jim accidently painted a white stripe down Treve's forehead.

Tom picked Mr Morris up from the airfield and brought him down to the stables. By this time Treve was over in the corner of the yard. The stallion wandered towards the two men, who were talking to each another, when suddenly Mr Morris turned around, looked at Treve, and then went right off.

'I've been had! I didn't buy a baldy horse,' he exclaimed. Baldy horses have thick white stripes down their foreheads.

Tom walked off in disgust as Jim tried to explain to Mr Morris exactly what had happened to Treve.

Just then, around the corner came Lynn and Sabu, riding flat out on the two precious, expensive new thoroughbred colts, almost knocking Tom and Mr Morris over. Tom said to his boss, 'I try to keep these boys out in the stock camp. That way they only get into half as much trouble.'

17

The engagement party

It was February and Ralph was *still* at Limbunya. Heavy rain had been falling off and on since November. Every time Ralph attempted to come back to Wave for our engagement party, the Victoria River or Gills Creek would be the deterrent.

One morning at breakfast, Tom Fisher suddenly announced, 'I think this weekend we'll all head over to Limbunya for the engagement party.'

Great excitement! The whole station started preparing. Graham Johnson, the droving overseer, had gone on holidays and very conveniently left his truck at Wave Hill. The following day we all piled into or onto the truck and Land Rover. On the way we picked up Molly and Basil, together with Jill and Ian Booth.

Limbunya Station was mostly open downs country, lightly timbered, and we passed a huge crater on the way. The buildings were new, shiny corrugated iron on short stilts, with big verandahs and surrounded by lawns and newly planted Poinciana trees.

When we reunited, Ralph and I felt embarrassed with everyone looking on. I was also aware that Heather Russell and Betty Crabbe, the two bookkeepers at Limbunya, had been getting on extremely well with Ralph: I think I was a bit jealous. However, everyone had come for an engagement party, including me, and that's what we were going to have.

Self-consciously, Ralph presented me with a beautiful sapphire and diamond ring, which we'd selected together from the catalogue of an Adelaide jeweller.

Formalities over, the two of us were able to relax and enjoy ourselves in the supportive company of our friends. It was a thoroughly fun party.

The next day the boys got into hijinks on the lawn. Trying to outdo one another, they engaged in feats of strength, somersaults, press-ups and arm-wrestling, all of which amazed and amused me.

Then the time came for us to head back and, sadly, Ralph and I were again parted. I had to leave him in the company of those two lovely girls!

Congratulatory telegrams from friends and family in Wollongong, Vancouver and Sydney were waiting for me on my arrival at Wave.

It was exciting—but I longed for my fiancé's return.

18

The horse muster

Late in February Tom Fisher asked me if I'd like to come on the horse muster. I said yes—but I didn't know what I was in for! I hadn't been on a horse since I'd fallen off Codeine in Lynn's camp. Grabbing a blanket and pillow and a change of clothes, plus the old toothbrush, I joined Tom and we drove out to the Ferguson Paddock near Mount Possum, south of the station.

All four camps were ready and waiting. Tom's horse and mine—Codeine!—were being saddled up. I walked up to Codeine, rubbed her nose gently and, as I stroked her neck, whispered, 'Please behave, Codeine . . . please, like a good girl.'

I desperately wanted to learn how to ride, and I didn't want to be a nuisance, asking for advice all the time. So up I got and we were off. I rode with Gunna and Colin. After two hours that felt like twenty, my bum had become very tender from bouncing up and down in the saddle.

Then I saw Lynn galloping towards me. 'Put the weight on your bloody feet,' he called, 'not on your arse!' And he was gone.

What a difference it made. With my weight on my feet, I could even stand up in the stirrups. We were mustering through these huge horse paddocks, very rough in parts with rugged hills interspersed with stony creeks, masses of water to cross, and thick scrub.

All the stock camp staff were required there that day to ensure a successful muster. We found dozens of horses and they seemed to know the right thing to do as we pushed them on. I was feeling quite exhausted and couldn't wait for the lunchbreak. How I was going to ride all afternoon, I didn't know.

I've never been so pleased to see the end of a day. When we arrived back at our camp, I was feeling like death. Sitting around the campfire, eating stew and damper and drinking billy tea made us all feel much better.

As beautiful as it was to sit under a stunningly starlit sky, chatting by the glow of the campfire, we all soon retired, exhausted. My bed was just a patch of dirt about twenty metres from the fire. I tried lying on my side, then on my back. I got up and dug a hole for my hip. I literally tossed and turned all night—was I glad to see the dawn! An early cup of billy tea was the rejuvenator to get us all going again.

The horses were brought back to the station yard where Tom Fisher drafted the 'horse plants': five horses to a man, plus five to be used exclusively for night watch of the cattle. This meant that they were tied to a tree at night with their saddles and bridles on in case of an emergency such as a cattle rush, when the beasts get a fright and literally stampede, taking everything in their path.

At the mustering, the mares, foals, geldings and pensioners all went through the round yard to determine their status and then were sorted out. Foals were weaned and branded, and castrated if appropriate. Mares were allocated to a particular stallion's paddock. Pensioners were put together in their own paddock to end their days in retirement after years of hard work.

Each stock camp took its horses for the season. One by one, the animals were ridden in the round yard to see how well they bucked. The really dynamic buckjump horses were kept for the upcoming annual rodeo at the Negri Races. The young colts were ridden every day and sometimes tied to the mules and led around against their will; this helped to quieten them. The quieter horses went to the young horse tailors or the older men, while the rough horses ended up being stock horses or were used to pull the stock-camp buggy.

The next job was to shoe every horse, and this took a few days. A three-quarter circular steel plate was nailed to the outer shell of the hoof to protect it from rough stony ground.

Before going from the yard out to the stock camps, the pack mules and horses had to be tied up and loaded with food rations, coarse salt for the corn beef, a bag of sugar, camp ovens, billy cans, an anvil, spare horse shoes, and swags of clothes and toiletry items. Usually there was one pack animal per person in the camp.

Each camp had its own buggy drawn by horses or mules to carry everything else the staff needed. There would be four to six mules or horses harnessed into the shafts of the buggy. On board lay a great heap of gear—swags, utensils, saddlery—and bags of potatoes, onions and salted meat. And sitting on top there'd be a favourite cattle dog, the cook and some of the horse tailors.

Once the stockmen were ready on their horses, off they went to their respective camps.

19

The drover

Ralph finally returned to Wave Hill in April. It was wonderful to have him back and be able to talk about our future together. While he'd been away I'd started to have some doubts. Were we really made for each other? He was gone for three months, longer than the time I had known him. But when he came back, I knew I loved him and it was all meant to be.

Not long after, the drover Mick Coombes, with four Aboriginal stockmen, came to Wave Hill to take three hundred head of bullocks. Mick and his men would be bringing them across the Murranji Track and down to Helen Springs Station. Here they'd be fattened before moving on to Queensland. The Murranji Track, sometimes called 'the ghost road of the drovers', was a travelling stock route or authorised thoroughfare for the walking of livestock from one location to another. It was pioneered by Nat Buchanan in 1881, as was the Barkly Stock Route.

The night before Mick and his team were due to leave, we all went out to Schules Yard, eight kilometres away, to watch the cattle through the night, before handing them over to the drover the following day. This was to get the beasts in practice for staying together and to help prevent a rush.

In pairs, we took turns walking our horses around the mob of cattle. I went with Ralph, of course, riding Codeine who behaved herself. It was imperative to keep the mob quiet, no disruptions, so we sang quietly as we worked.

Only Tony refused to sing: 'I've got a lousy voice.'

'Hear, hear,' everyone agreed.

So he recited one of Will Ogilvie's poems from *Saddle for a Throne* instead.

The atmosphere of the stock camp captured the true heart of the Territory for me. In the camp, on a beautiful moonlit night, there was the gentle lowing of the cattle, the jangle of the Condamine bells around the necks of the mules, the Aboriginal stockmen chanting in their native tongue, and dear old Codeine plodding along in time to their rhythm. Around the flickering campfire, the boys would be telling stories.

Ralph told an incredible collection of hilarious outback tales involving people, animals and birds. We had to control our laughter in case we caused a stampede.

The next day the drover and his men left with the herd, and we wished them luck. They needed it: there was one vital water source on the Murranji Track. If the droving team found that it was dry, they had a 177-kilometre trek to reach water. That was why their stock route was considered the worst of all.

This would have been one of the last droving trips from Wave Hill, as road trains took over in 1965.

20

Wedding at Limbunya

Rod Russell, one of our stockmen, was transferred to Limbunya just before Ralph's return. Rod became quite smitten by Heather the bookkeeper. Not long after this bit of gossip reached us there came word of their engagement. Then Ralph and I had a letter asking if we would be bridesmaid and best man.

The Australian Inland Mission padre, Stuart Lang, married Heather and Rod. Ray and Pat Jansen, the managers of Limbunya, hosted the wedding. Quite a few of the boys from Wave came over with us, together with Molly and Basil, our friends from the police station, and old Clarrie Wilkinson.

Clarrie was a retired Vestey manager. He'd worked on most of the properties in the Territory and the Kimberley since 1914. He was eighty years of age when I met him, and Vestey allowed him to stay on any station he chose for as long as he liked. He was a mine of knowledge about the region and the company properties. Around the Ord River in one year he'd supposedly shot fourteen thousand brumbies and feral donkeys. He told great stories about the old days.

One of the stations he'd managed was Sturt Creek, ninety kilometres south-west of Wave. Clarrie told us about the homestead being made of stone with six- by six-inch holes in the walls at shoulder height: enough space to allow a gun to be fired out, but not enough for a spear to be thrown inside.

The wedding at Limbunya was a very happy affair—a beautiful bride, a touching service—and at the end Clarrie announced in a loud voice, 'She's got the hobbles on him now!'

Ralph and I were very impressed by Heather and Rod's sensible decision to get married on the station without all the hoo-ha of a wedding down south, which we'd have had to organise from the Territory. The couple then spent their honeymoon at the Negri Races in Western Australia.

Back at Wave Hill there was no more time to think about weddings—the races were nearly upon us! We were expecting important visitors. John, Lord Vestey's cousin, had been a jackaroo under Tom Fisher at Wave Hill, and he was coming over to introduce his Australian-born wife, Gay.

I was quite horrified at the proposed accommodation in the visitors' quarters for our VIPs. Most of the rooms were like dormitories, with steel beds lined up along the walls. There was only one that was at all suitable, and it had walls of flywire gauze! I decided to curtain these walls with material out of the store. Not a great choice was available: head cloth or floral seersucker. Luckily the latter looked pretty against three of the walls.

Unlike everyone else, Tom wasn't so keen on the Negri Races. A couple of years earlier, as starter of the horses, he'd been insulted by Tommie Swan, an old employer of the Vestey stations, who'd said, 'Tom, you couldn't start a mob of chooks off a roost.' Since then he'd refused to go back and wouldn't allow any of his staff to attend either, until that year.

Before arriving, John had let Tom know that he'd love to go to the famous races, as he had never been before, so Tom gave in and lifted his ban. Most of the staff took off for the Negri the day before John and Gay landed, leaving Ralph, Tom and I to host that morning. Ralph and I were soon allowed to take our leave, while Tom promised our guests that he'd bring them over the following day.

21

My first Negri

I'd heard so much about previous Negri Races that I was curious and excited to find out for myself how they worked. The Negri was one of the best picnic race meetings in the north, with horses put into training months beforehand. They were grass-fed: no grain was to be given to them. However, a few trainers didn't follow the rules and this upset the honest ones.

Each station had its own race camp. My first year, Wave Hill's camp was one big bough shed with a tarpaulin roof to accommodate about fifteen people, divided into small rooms with walls of branches. Some weeks before, one or two of the stock camps had been sent over to set everything up. The stockmen had cleared our campsite of long grass, put spinifex and branches around the walls of the bough shed, and collected firewood. Every year improvements were made to the facilities. In later years we had hessian for walls instead of branches. The camps became bigger, with large dining-room, kitchen and barbecue areas, and separate bough sheds for married couples, single women and single men.

In 1961, the racecourse was around twenty kilometres from another Vestey property, Ord River Station, near the Linacre River: 240 kilometres from Wave Hill. Earlier the races had been held near the Negri River, hence the name. These sites are in the same area as the Bungle Bungles, where the spectacular eroded remains of a mountain range now attracts thousands of tourists every year.

I was the only woman in the Wave race camp that first year, and my room was next to old Clarrie Wilkinson's. Every morning he'd awaken us with, 'Who's for a nip of rum?' That was the start of his day, each day at the races.

On the first evening of the week-long race meeting, Ralph and I went up to the bar area where a refrigerated truck loaded with alcohol had just arrived from Wyndham. All the men were there, but Ralph bypassed them to take me over to where the women were chatting. We were warmly welcomed by these lovely ladies, most of whom were managers' wives: Robin Hill, Mary Jones, Mrs McLachlan, Pat Jansen, Dawn Watts, Peg Underwood from Inverway, and others I can't recall. I was introduced to them all. Then Ralph said, 'I'll see you later!'

'You're not going to leave me here,' I said. 'I want to go to the bar with you and have a drink.'

He was horrified. 'You have to stay with the women. You can't come drinking with the men!' He started to walk away. Just then Graham Fulcher, who worked on Ord River Station, came along with his fiancée, Robyn Kirk, also from Sydney.

Robyn felt the same as me. We didn't want to be anti-social towards the women, but we did want to enjoy the company of our menfolk on that first evening.

We started a new trend: *Women can drink at the bar with the men!*

Tom brought John and Gay Vestey over to the races the following day, but they stayed at Ord River Station. During the course of John's visit, the boys pinched his rather pucker velour Akubra, and each station's custom-designed branding earmark was clipped into its brim. The hat looked a masterpiece. Unfortunately the boys got nervous about the possible con-sequences, so they threw the hat in the campfire. John was so disappointed when he found out, as it would have been a great memento of his trip to all the Vestey stations.

Prior to the Negri each year, the men trained the horses and did the station work while the women prepared their outfits for the two days of races. Fashion dictated that gloves and hats were to be worn, with those fabulous outfits bought in Sydney or Perth, or wherever they'd visited on their previous holiday. And not to be forgotten were additional outfits for the two-day rodeo, the Calcutta night, the Negri Ball and the award presentation night.

In the early days we danced to taped music, but later when the race meeting became bigger and grander we hired a talented DJ who played fabulous music. We would rock and roll, do the Twist, the Stomp, the Shuffle—whatever the latest dance craze was, we were into it.

There was also much entertaining in the different camps, with each trying to outdo the others. The women planned the menus well before hosting these events—cereal or steak and eggs for breakfast, corn beef or roast and salad for lunch, and plenty of stews and curries or a barbecue for dinner.

The Negri wasn't only for the whites; all the Aboriginal families came, too. They camped around our camps, helped in the kitchens and dining rooms, and looked after the children. They all loved the races and catching up with 'relation alonga me', but not 'cousin'.

Meanwhile, hawker vans would set up with their displays of shirts, trousers, dresses and hats, attracting much attention. These vans had lift-up sides with sections to show off the clothing. There were racks to hang and examine clothes on, as well as boxes of boots and leather-gear like halters. The hawkers also carried men's hats, belts, buckles, penknives, liniments—practically anything a bushman would require.

The first hawkers in the Territory were the Afghan cameleers, small numbers of immigrants with their 'ships of the desert'. Darwin to Adelaide, as they say in the Outback, is a bloody long way. No one was very keen to cross it. That is, until the Afghan cameleers arrived and set about opening up Australia's Red Centre. Their legacy: the million-odd camels that now plague the Outback, plus the name of the epic rail journey crossing the continent from south to north, The Ghan.

There were six or seven races over two days at the Negri, including the main races, the Cup and the Bracelet. There were races for Aboriginal jockeys and even a ladies' race. Bets were put on with the bookmakers as the jockeys paraded their horses in front of the grandstand before trotting off to the starting line.

As well as the horseraces, there was the campdraft, flag race, barrel race and pickup, followed by foot races, throwing the broom and tug of war. The highlight for the Aboriginal attendees was the rodeo with its bullock rides, bareback bronco rides and buckjumping.

We all loved it.

22

Our wedding

Not long after we returned from the Negri, Father John Flynn, the Catholic priest from Darwin, came on his rounds. He'd been an eye specialist before he was ordained and ironically he had developed an eye condition that caused his teardrops to dry up. Father Flynn invented an ingenious attachment for his glasses: a small rubber flask filled with water was fitted to each arm, with tubing that when squeezed would spray a jet of water into each eye.

At the time of Father Flynn's visit, my mother was overseas and not due home for months. Ralph and I, being very much in love and anxious to get married, decided to talk to Father Flynn about wanting to be together. He was a lovely, caring man with a great sense of humour. Heather and Rod's wedding had made us think, *Why wait until we go to Sydney for our holidays to marry?* That was months away.

We'd planned to have a big wedding at Edgecliff in Sydney's eastern suburbs the following January. The venue, the bridesmaids: all had been decided upon. Much organising was needed and we were so far away.

Also, the way everyone at the station looked at us was irritating—they presumed we were having a love affair, which was right in one way, but without the sex. I wanted to remain a virgin until I married. The problem was that despite being a good Catholic girl, I was finding it impossible to resist Ralph's loving advances. What if I succumbed? What if I became pregnant? Even though I was a nurse, I knew nothing about contraceptives.

Confessions were heard and mass was said on the paperbark verandah, and then we confided in Father Flynn. He gave us his blessing: he would marry us. This was the answer! My mother not being there was the only flaw, but I knew she would understand. The next thing we knew, we were having a wedding. There was no mucking around in the Territory— things just happened.

The event took only a few days to organise. Ralph and I did nothing except give the postmistress, Nancy Walton, a guest list of people from the area plus Ralph's mother, Mary 'Cudge' Connors, who was at Mount Bundy near Katherine.

Father Flynn, a very persuasive man, talked Ralph into becoming a Catholic. This was relatively easy for him because he'd spent half his childhood in Catholic schools in Alice and Brisbane: his mother's choice, which seemed strange as Squizzy Taylor, Mary's father, hated Catholics. But a year later, when I nervously met him and Grandma Taylor in Brisbane, we got on like a house on fire.

Everyone else organised the wedding. Nancy sent the invitations via telegram. The policeman's wife, Molly, donated the wedding dress and made the cake. The settlement school-teacher, Jill Booth, loaned the veil. Some food was brought by the women guests, the majority being served by the station kitchen. The alcohol was ordered and collected from Top Springs.

The smoko verandah was turned into a church with branches strategically placed around the walls. Chairs were arranged in rows with an aisle up the middle lined with red mats from the store. The front seat from a jeep, covered with a white sheet, was used for the bridal pair to kneel on. A table from the bookkeeper's office, covered with a white damask tablecloth, served as the altar.

My bridesmaids were Lauris Farrow, the bookkeeper's wife, together with Sandra and Alison, English girls who were visiting the station at the time. Mandy Warren, Joy and Jim's daughter from Cattle Creek, was the flower girl. Ralph's best man was Tony Clark, and the groomsmen were his brother Lynn and his childhood friend Sabu Singh. Ralph's mother flew in with her second husband, Jack Connors, and helped with much of the organising.

Two nights before the wedding, a bucks party was organised at the station and the hens was to be at the police station. Ralph found out before we girls left for the party that someone was planning to play a joke by locking the main gate between us and the police station. Thankfully Ralph gave me an extra key—as it turned out, we needed it. We didn't let on to anyone that we'd had any trouble getting through, which would have puzzled the culprit!

Bill Walton, the mechanic, provided the vehicle, which was black and gleaming and drove me from my donga to the homestead entrance, all of a hundred yards. Tom was waiting to escort me down the aisle and give me away. He was looking very serious and asked, 'How are you feeling?'

'Wonderful,' I replied.

My only regret was that my dear mother wasn't there. She was in the middle of the Atlantic on a cruise liner drinking our health—so her cable said—and I felt very guilty. Sorry, Mum!

Tom and I walked down the cobblestone path onto the smoko verandah with all the Wave Hill mob, family and friends eager to see me and Ralph hitched. I felt like a princess. Ralph looked very handsome and appeared quite nervous. But Father Flynn took control, performing a beautiful wedding service followed by the nuptial mass, with Ralph receiving his first Holy Communion.

Photos were taken in the courtyard, which would have been great except it was very late in the afternoon and the shadows were strong. At that stage, however, we didn't give it a thought. We just wanted to get the formalities over so the party could begin!

The reception was held in the dining room. There were too many people for the number of chairs, so only the bridal party sat down. The wedding cake made by Molly Courts was the star attraction on the table, which was gorgeously set with well-laundered white tablecloths. The guests ate buffet-style and stood around the table. When the party started, the champagne and beer flowed. We danced to Johnny Cash and a collection of donated records.

We'd been offered accommodation for the night down at the schoolteacher's house. We were reluctant to leave our fantastic party for the settlement, but we thought it wise if we were to have any peace.

The next morning we drove back to the station to find the party still going. We joined everyone for a beer on the smoko verandah. This was still decked out in eucalyptus branches and flowers. The chairs were still lined up as in a chapel.

23

The honeymoon

Having packed our gear, said our farewells and thanks, we started off for Darwin on our honeymoon. Pat Bellamy, the bore mechanic, lent us his Holden sedan, so we felt very grand setting off on the Buchanan Highway for Katherine, 460 kilometres away. We had one passenger—a man from Wave who needed a lift.

It took us twelve hours to get to Manbullo Station as we were confronted with miles of bulldust in which we got bogged several times. Having had the experience of getting bogged on the way to Ayres Rock, I shared my knowledge of putting branches under the wheels to get us out. But I think it was more our pushing that did the trick, and we were helped by our passenger.

We spent the night at Manbulloo on the banks of the Katherine River. In Katherine, Ralph took me to meet Anna and Ted 'Cowboy' Collins, who at that stage lived in town. Later they moved to a property a few kilometres out, and named it

Uralla after the town in the NSW Tablelands where Cowboy was born.

Years earlier, Cowboy had been the postman for the outlying properties, delivering all the mail by packhorse. One story he told us was about taking a dozen hats to the ladies on the stations in readiness for the yearly races. Cowboy said the hatboxes were very difficult to tie on to his saddles; they kept dislodging and falling to the ground. He got sick of this, so he opened all the boxes, took out the hats and jammed them into just two boxes. Imagine the ladies' faces when they saw their beautiful hats!

Ralph and I continued on to Darwin, where we spent a week at the Old Vic, a lovely brick and stone hotel in the main shopping strip. The Old Vic was also the main 'watering hole': the most popular pub in Darwin. We could also have stayed in the Don Hotel or the Darwin Hotel, but as Ralph had chosen it I just went where Ralph took me.

Ralph told me about how in December 1941, he, his mother and two brothers—all of them living at Waterloo Station—were compulsorily evacuated from Darwin by ship. That year, soldiers who had boarded SS *Zealandia* in Darwin to go south on their holidays suddenly had their leave cancelled with the news of the bombing of Pearl Harbor. Everyone in Darwin became very anxious. War was looming on Australia's doorstep. Most of the women and children were compulsorily evacuated from all over the Northern Territory. Darwin was bombed in February 1942, the first of many bombing raids.

Darwin in 1961 had a very 'country town' feel about it. The population was about thirty to forty thousand. But after twelve months on the station it still seemed like a big bustling city. I was desperate for some decent clothes, so shopping was a priority; I'd only had a few changes of clothes when I first arrived at Wave Hill. My mother had sent me several items, but this was my first chance to shop in nearly a year. As I tried them on, Ralph would say, impatiently, 'Yes, buy that one. Yes, that's attractive, buy that and that, and *that* one.' I didn't mind. Ralph seemed to be getting such a kick at my pleasure in trying on all these clothes. I had never bought more than one dress at a time and here was my gorgeous husband encouraging me to have half a dozen while he proudly paid the bill.

We were so enjoying ourselves, walking around holding hands, which we would have been too embarrassed to do at Wave Hill. We just revelled in being on our own without everyone on the station looking on. After a wonderful week in Darwin it was time to return to work. Word had spread that we were on the road, and old friends of Ralph's, the Keegan brothers, hailed us down. These work-hard, play-hard stockmen had spent many years in the Territory. They insisted we stop and have a drink—no, not just one, but two or three. I hated beer so I was off the hook. When we finally drove away—no breathalysers in those days!—the Keegan brothers followed us. Thirty kilometres down the road, they passed us, hailed us down and insisted that the bridegroom partake of another beer. We were getting sick of this, so Ralph put his foot down. We politely left them and sped away.

*

Back at Wave, we settled into married life while living in the sister's donga plus a caravan that Gus Ringler, the Vestey improvement manager, and his wife, Pat, had lived in while waiting for their house to be built at Nicholson, another Vestey station just over the border in Western Australia.

My just-married days were spent studying *Mrs Beeton's Cookery Book*, my engagement present from Tom Fisher; practising my cooking on Ralph, the poor fellow; and playing house, which I loved, while continuing with the nursing, housekeeping and hostessing.

As a young girl I used to go with my mother and grandmother when they had their hairdressing appointments. For our yearly ballet concerts I was allowed to have my hair set with butterfly clips, hairpins or rollers. I would think, *Maybe I should become a hairdresser*. At Wave Hill, I finally did. Starting with Ralph and the boys, I graduated to cutting my house girls' hair. They all had good heads of hair, making any style possible. It was fun, but I'm glad I didn't do it for a living!

24

Back to Sydney

Holidays came every two years with two months' holiday pay and a return airfare. At the end of 1961, Ralph's holidays were due, together with quite a few of the boys'. We flew to Sydney, then on to Wollongong to my mother's unit on Cliff Road. The weather was beautiful and we spent a lot of time on the beach. We caught up with my family and friends, all of whom were eager to meet Ralph.

We booked into Kanimbla Hall at Kings Cross to meet up with our Territory mates and my Sydney friends. The latter were dying to meet my shy, handsome cattleman. We went out to the most stylish nightclubs—places like Romano's and Prince's— where we dined and danced until the wee small hours. We tried new restaurants, took in a few movies and even went to an opera. We decided to have a really big party and invite everyone we knew from the Territory and Sydney.

It was a great party, but became a bit wild when someone threw a beer bottle into the back seat of a guest's MG, parked just outside. What a commotion, with many drunken heads leaning out of the second-floor windows, yelling and carrying on at two o'clock in the morning. The last guests left the flat around 3 a.m. There was a terrible mess—empty beer bottles, overflowing ashtrays, and dirty glasses and plates everywhere! We were exhausted but knew we had to leave in the morning, so we cleaned up before we retired.

Thank goodness we did! At the crack of dawn there was a hammering on our door. It was the manager of Kanimbla Hall asking or, rather, *telling* us that he would like us to leave as soon as possible. We were quite shocked—we'd never been thrown out of any place before!

Ralph went back to the Territory without me, as I was expecting our first child. I went and stayed with my mother in Wollongong. Mum's next-door neighbour, a Royal Prince Alfred graduate, gave me all sorts of good advice on baby matters, and I started to look at the situation from the patient's point of view.

Mum and I moved to Sydney two weeks before I was due at Crown Street Women's Hospital. I was exactly on time. Boy, those labour pains were so strong! The baby got stressed and I ended up having a forceps delivery. Normally at Crown Street, a forceps delivery meant that the baby went straight into the nursery, with the mother not seeing her baby until the next day. But when my gorgeous obstetrician, Dr James MacBeth, was free from deliveries, he went down to the nursery, picked up my newborn baby, Anthony John Hayes, and brought him up to my room.

There are moments in life that are so fantastic that you never forget them. One of them for me was seeing our first-born child. He was so beautiful and so alert I could not believe that Ralph and I had created such a gorgeous creature.

It was such an exciting time: taking care of a new baby, receiving telegrams from so many in the Territory, having my Sydney friends come to visit us.

As a registered nurse and a midwife, I'd looked after nurseries full of babies, but there was no way I was going back to Wave Hill before I knew exactly how to feed and look after little Anthony. I went to the Tresillian Home for Mothers and Babies at Point Piper. My time there was invaluable. The nurses trained the babies to sleep nearly all night. Any breastfeeding problems were taken care of, and information was given on weaning and care. By the time we left I was quite confident about going back to the Outback with a baby.

Prior to returning to meet his dad, Anthony was christened in Wollongong with a few family members and friends present.

From the time I'd gone south to have my baby, the company had hired another nursing sister to work temporarily in my place. When I returned to the station, I was offered the job of postmistress because Bill and Nancy Walton had moved on. However, the mail plane came at one o'clock every Thursday afternoon, and that was when I started my third breastfeed for the day. So there was no way I would take on the job—nothing could interrupt that!

Ralph and I and our baby were now living in Tom Fisher's quarters. Tom had moved to the post office cottage when the

Waltons left. My days were filled with looking after Anthony, but I would go to morning and afternoon smoko to catch up with everyone and to show off our beautiful child.

Ralph had organised a meat-safe cot for Anthony. The whole top was encased in gauze, so there were no worries about mosquitoes or flies. He looked so tiny in it! Emilie, our house girl in our new quarters, loved looking after Anthony while doing the housework and washing. I was really spoilt.

One day I received a parcel from my mother. It was a delightful cotton dress with a gathered skirt of bright red, orange and yellow squares. But Ralph took one look at it and said, 'That's too bright for you. You can't wear that.'

So, to keep him happy, I said to Emilie, 'Who should I give this dress to?'

It was a size ten.

'Please, Missus, give him me.'

'But it won't fit you,' I said, Emilie being a considerably larger size.

'No, Missus, me fix him up.' Off Emilie went with the dress.

Several hours later she returned, resplendent in her new dress. Every seam, every gathering had been let out and sewn by hand—and it fitted.

In the weeks that followed, 'the dress' was seen on at least ten different Aboriginal girls around the place—at the settlement, at Limbunya Station, and even as far away as Nicholson.

25

Twins

A few months later I was back doing the nursing on the station.

Sister Ellen Kettle, the rural survey sister in the Territory, notified us that she was doing a tour of the stations and settlements where registered nurses were employed. She would be arriving the following week. I knew that Sister Kettle had started a register of Aboriginal births and infant deaths in the Territory. The old galvanised clinic with its cement floors got an extra spring clean that week.

Anthony was three months old at this stage and Ralph was going to be out in the stock camp. Tom was on holidays.

Sister Kettle duly arrived. I took her down to the clinic and we went through a lot of my records. She was there for my morning appointments. That afternoon we continued with more patients, and then around 4.30 p.m. Ida came into the hospital to say that Marian, a young Aboriginal woman, had had her baby. The routine was that after the birth, the mother—when she was feeling up to it—would bring the baby up to the hospital, and both would be checked over by the nursing sister. Mother and baby arrived; they were fine.

I said to Sister Kettle, 'I'm going to go and feed Anthony. See you at dinner.'

A little later, I'd just finished breastfeeding my son when there was an urgent knock at my door. It was Sister Kettle with two babies, one on each arm, wrapped in rather discoloured shawls.

'Thea,' she said, puffing and panting, 'you'll have to look after these two. They both belong to Marian. She's had twins. After you left the clinic, Pansy came up to tell me that the elders of the tribe were going to get rid of one of the babies.'

And off she went to dinner! I didn't know where Marian was, but I wished Sister Kettle had brought her up too. I'm not sure whether I ate that night; probably not, as we all ate in the dining room and I don't think the boys would have thought of me. If Ralph had been there instead of out in the camp, it would have been a different story.

There I was with three babies who woke every hour—including Anthony, who normally woke only once per night—and I had to feed them. Thank goodness I had a few baby bottles, so the twins could drink boiled water. I kept thinking, *Where's Marian?* Then I thought, *Lucky woman—Sister Kettle probably chased her back to the camp last night.*

The next morning I struggled down to the dining room, having instructed Emilie to find Marian urgently so that she could feed her babies. This left Pansy in charge of the 'nursery', while I breakfasted with a well-rested Sister Kettle.

'How are they, Thea?'

'Well, they're fine but very hungry. Hopefully Marion is on her way now.'

There was no mention of how was I after a night of horror with no sleep, up every hour to calm three screaming babies.

Sister Kettle had to move on to her next port of call, which would have been the Wave Hill settlement, so we said goodbye, with the sister adding, 'I do think you should keep those babies under your care, as you never know what would happen to them in a big hospital.'

I didn't argue with her, because it didn't really matter where Marian went with her babies. The fate of one of the twins was inevitable with the tribal laws as they were.

Once I saw Sister Kettle's vehicle going out the gate, I got on to the Aerial Medical Service and told them I had two premature babies for them to pick up with their mother. Some weeks later, poor Marian returned with only one child. The other had died of a chest infection. As Ralph said, the baby would not have survived in the camp if it had returned anyway.

Over the following years, I learnt more about Ellen Kettle, this nursing sister and historian. She, with Dr John Hargreaves, compiled the first register of leprosy patients in Australia. Ellen also wrote her autobiography, *Gone Bush*, which gives a remarkable insight into the work of this dedicated and courageous woman. She received an MBE for her work with Aboriginal people.

26

My second Negri

In 1962 my mother came to see her first grandchild again and accompany us to the Negri Races. Ralph, who loved old cars, had bought a Humber Super Snipe on holidays and driven it back to Wave Hill. A luxurious English car with rich-looking leather upholstery, it was a few years old, shiny black, and looked a bit like a Rolls Royce. It was a beautiful car but not suited to dusty conditions.

We drove our Humber to the races and it was bulldusty to say the least: a worry with a baby, but we coped. On the way we called in to Inverway Station to see Peg and Pat Underwood. They were a hospitable couple who loved the races and usually did very well with their racehorses.

The Negri was a real eye-opener for Mum: her first time camping in a bush donga and seeing a bush race meeting. The rodeo and campdrafting fascinated her. The thing that she couldn't get over was the quantity of alcohol consumed. She even asked the barman how many cartons of beer and bottles of spirits he'd ordered, and then recorded it in her diary. She would go on to delight in telling her friends in Wollongong all about the enormous amount of alcohol.

The Vestey Company declared it was time to upgrade the buildings for both whites and Aboriginals at Wave Hill. As Ralph and I had just been married, the company decided that the first building would be an overseer's cottage. Vestey hired the 'Greek boys' to come out from Katherine to build our house. They were good builders but bad lads, as they would bring bottles of potent ouzo out for Tom Fisher and probably some of the men in the kitchen.

When the cottage was completed, Ralph and I suggested to Tom that, as he was the manager, he should move in. '*Karjinga*,' Tom's favourite Gurindji expletive, 'what would I want with a flash house like that?'

So we very happily moved into our three-bedroom cottage with a lounge/dining room, kitchen, pantry and closed-in verandah. The highlight of our home was the septic toilet with its push-button flush, situated inside just off the bathroom—no more going out in the dark to find the loo, no more sitting on a stinking thunderbox!

Unfortunately, the overseer's cottage had been built right beside the old men's quarters. Our bedroom had floor-to-ceiling windows looking straight out onto these quarters. I asked Tom about curtains for the cottage, and particularly for our bedroom, but he showed no interest as he was always conscious of the budget. We ended up hanging our queen-size sheets, received as a wedding present, over our windows.

By the time our cottage was completed, the company realised there wasn't enough water on the present site. Building ceased. The Greek boys left. Messrs Peter Morris and Reginald Durack flew down to Wave Hill and decided that the perfect site for a new station complex was near the settlement. The complex was to sit atop a range of basalt hills with contoured banks that look like waves rolling down from top to bottom: this is where Wave Hill got its name.

Water was needed and so a boring contractor, Jack Warner, was employed to start drilling with a percussion drill at the new site. It was a great scenic spot high up on the hills, but not a place for gardens, and it was far too close to the settlement.

Molly and Basil were transferred to Tennant Creek, and a new policeman and his wife, Roy and Margaret Harvey, took over. We were invited down to the police station for dinner one Saturday night not long after they arrived. As we sat out in the breezeway of their house, socialising, all very pleasant, I was thinking what a well-organised hostess Margaret was, with no dashing to and from the kitchen to check on the cooking. Suddenly she said, 'Okay, Roy, are you ready to cook?'

Off he went and returned some time later with a tray covered in barbecued rib bones. Ray and I loved ribs but these were about half a metre long. We sat there eating with one hand on each end of the bone. It was hilarious; I thought, *I'm really in the bush now!*

Margaret told a story about her two house girls, Mildred and Connie, who'd also worked for Molly and Basil. One day

Margaret threw out the David Jones catalogue, which she had
no more use for. The two girls found it in the rubbish bin and got
very excited when they saw 'all dem pretty clothes'. Margaret
offered to buy anything they wanted.

'Yes, Missus, we want trouser alonga *noberloo*.'

They wanted bras—padded ones at that. Margaret tried to
talk them out of it, as they were quite big girls. But that was
what they wanted, so Margaret ordered the padded bras.

Sometime later, after the bras had arrived and been given to
Mildred and Connie, Roy and Margaret decided to go fishing
up the river and brought the trackers and house girls. They were
all scattered along the riverbank, and Roy walked over to see
how the girls were going catching yabbies.

He came back to Margaret and said, 'Come have a look
at this!'

There were the girls, pulling up the yabbies, their hands
wrapped in the 'trousers along *noberloo*'—one side under the
yabby and one side on top—to protect their skin from the claws.

27

The Americans

Tom married a lovely Irish lady, Anne, whom he'd met in his hometown of Kyogle. Once again we insisted that Tom move into the new house, with his new bride—but no. 'We've settled into the post office cottage and there we will stay,' he told us.

One evening, Tom and Anne decided to have drinks at their place, as they had visitors, the Jansens from Limbunya. I left Anthony in the care of Pansy while Ralph and I went over to their cottage.

Anne poured the drinks; we were all drinking Scotch with dry ginger or soda. Instead of a nip of Scotch in a glass of soft drink, Anne served the reverse! We all got pie-eyed, so much so that the party ended quite quickly and everyone staggered home to bed. It was the last time we allowed Anne to pour our drinks.

Australian beef producers were looking for export markets; America was after more hamburger beef for their fast-food outlets. A member of the Australian Trade Commission knew Tom Fisher and arranged to bring a plane-load of Texan ranchers and their wives to Wave Hill to see some good-quality Shorthorn cattle.

The Americans were to arrive in a Douglas DC-3, a fixed-wing propeller-driven plane. The plan was for them to have the day at Wave and then fly on to the town of Kununurra for the night.

The day before their arrival, the Greek boys, who'd recently moved to the police station, passed through Wave bringing a cargo of grog. They called in to see Anne and Tom with bottles of ouzo.

Early the next morning, I went down to the homestead to check on the smoko area and the dining room. Were there enough chairs? Enough place settings at the tables? Was everything clean and tidy? Ralph then informed me that Tom hadn't turned up for breakfast—most unusual.

Suddenly Anne arrived, looking quite distraught. 'Thea, please come have a look at Tom—he's very sick.'

Up at the post office cottage, I found Tom trying to drag himself out of bed, looking ill and breathing heavily. He was *very* hung-over; I'd seen him like this before.

'I'm a'right,' he slurred. 'Anne's jus' carryin' on 'bout nothin'. Be down later to see th'Mericans.'

'No,' I said, 'please stay in bed, Tom—you're not well. We can look after the visitors. I'll come back later and see how you are.' Of course, I was really thinking, *Tom, please don't embarrass us all by coming down!*

The Americans

Tom had a habit of feeling inadequate when important visitors were expected, which resulted in him getting on the grog if any was available. His insecurities were ridiculous, as he was a great conversationalist and a very interesting individual—when he was sober.

The Americans duly arrived. Ralph and the stockmen drove out to the aerodrome in several vehicles to pick them up. The big Texan men wore their ten-gallon hats. The women were very stylish, flashing their huge diamond rings.

We had drinks on the paperbark verandah before going in to lunch. The Texans were fun people and easy to entertain. After lunch, the men were taken out on the run to view some cattle. The women returned to the verandah, searching for a cool spot to read or chat. They felt the severe heat, especially as there were no fans or air-conditioning; otherwise they were quite happy. I left them to go and feed Anthony.

Returning to the verandah an hour later, I heard a gasp from one of the women. She was gazing up the entrance path to the homestead. Everyone turned to look in the direction of the post office cottage.

There was our manager, weaving and staggering down the path, waving a bottle in his hand.

'*Karjinga*,' mumbled Tom, as he plonked himself down on a chair in the midst of the women. They all shrank as far from him as they could. Luckily, the men had just returned and the pilot announced that they were now to fly on to Kununurra. The women looked very relieved.

But Tom, inebriated as he was, didn't miss this. 'Sounds

a good idea,' he said. 'I'd like t'go to Kununurra, if there's room.'

Unfortunately there was a spare seat, so off they all went, Tom included.

The passengers boarded the plane while the pilot sent his estimated time of arrival—but he couldn't get through. He tried again, and again, while they were all getting hotter and hotter in the plane. The pilot then announced that he was unable to fly to Kununurra, as 'sunspots' were preventing communication on his radio. Sighing and with gasps of horror at the prospect of staying the night at Wave Hill, the Texans disembarked.

Tom had to be woken up. Stepping out of the plane, he looked down at the ground and said, 'Proper good country, this Kununurra.'

Happily for the Americans, the sunspots cleared up before they had to return to that 'dreaded station'. Tom was taken back to the homestead, and our visitors flew to the comfort of their hotel.

We all breathed a sigh of relief.

28

Relieving at Gordon Downs

Sometime in October, Tom called Ralph into his office to inform him that we were being sent over to Gordon Downs Station in the Kimberley, situated right up against the Northern Territory–Western Australian border. We were to manage the property for twelve weeks while its manager, Stan Jones, and his family went on holidays. We were so excited. This was another challenge and we were proud that Ralph was to be given this opportunity to relieve for another Vestey manager. I was also excited because I'd been told that Gordon Downs was a delightful station: after all, Wave was very basic.

Leaving Wave Hill at the end of November, we drove via Nicholson Station where we called in to see the managers, Robin and Len Hill. As a young stockman, Len had driven cattle down the Canning Stock Route and back in 1946, an experience he later wrote about in his book *Droving with Ben Taylor*. Robin and Len had been at Nicholson since 1949.

We also visited Gus and Pat Ringler on the outskirts of the

station complex. Gus, the improvement manager, had lent us his caravan the year before. He was of German descent and had come out to Australia after World War II, after having been a member of the Hitler Youth Movement and later a prisoner of war in America. He was a very interesting character. His delightful wife, who kept their aluminium and steel house spotless, was Ceylonese—they'd met on a ship going to England. Ralph was good friends with Gus and Pat, and over the years we spent a lot of time in their company, together with their two children.

Having said farewell, we continued to Gordon Downs Station, an area of about half a million hectares. We drove eighty-five kilometres across a black soil, treeless plain covered in Mitchell and Flinders grasses on the edge of the Tanami Desert. Suddenly the plain ended. The soil became red. Spinifex and an abundance of low mulga scrub added beauty to this new landscape.

'It's only desert,' Ralph said, after I exclaimed at the abrupt change and the beauty of our surroundings. I decided I liked desert country.

Gordon Downs was on the Tanami Desert Road, which eventually headed south to Alice Springs; not that you could see much road, as it was overgrown with yam bushes and mulga trees. It has since been diverted to come out near Halls Creek.

We drove on for another thirteen kilometres, and there was the homestead, like an oasis: a red-and-white two-storey house surrounded by lush lawns. Trees shaded outdoor tables and chairs, and water sparkled as it twirled from the sprinklers. The Aboriginal girls were waiting on the lawn to bring the smoko down from the kitchen. After Wave Hill, we thought we were in heaven.

Stan and Mary Jones had five children, and their governess, a young Swiss girl called Shauna, stayed on to do the cooking for us for the twelve weeks we were there. She loved experimenting with food and we loved eating it. Smoko, morning or afternoon, was either under the trellis beside the house or under the trees on the lawn. We even had fresh vegetables flown in, which Tom would never have allowed.

Soon after our return from Gordon Downs to Wave, the Vesteys held a managers' meeting there, which Messrs Peter Morris and Eric Durack attended. The young managers and stockmen would come up to our house each day when business was finished. They were dying to have a drink, but Tom was the only one who had some grog and they weren't likely to get any of that. Then, one afternoon, Ralph suddenly thought of my 'apple wine'.

Months before, in my fruit order from Katherine, I'd received some green, green apples. Mrs Beeton, in her *Cookery Book*, told me how to make wine out of them. I asked Ralph for a container and he brought me a large ceramic bottle that had held battery acid. We gave it a thorough cleaning-out, then filled it with apples and the rest of the ingredients.

After the boys started drinking my apple wine, I suddenly had doubts. I thought of the container and its former contents:

What if I killed them all? No way would I have any! But they all drank it, praised the wine and became quite merry. Thank goodness they survived.

29

The curtains

In May 1964 Tom told me and Ralph that the governor-general, Lord De L'Isle, was coming to visit Wave Hill. His daughter Catherine Sidney, a French maid and an aide-de-camp would be accompanying him. I knew before Tom asked me where they would be staying, as we had the only decent house on the station.

I told Tom that they could have the cottage, because I wouldn't be there. 'I'll be in Darwin giving birth to my second child,' I said.

For a reason I can't recall, Tom and Anne weren't going to be at Wave either, so they asked the manager's wife from Nicholson Station, Robin Hill, to come over and act as hostess. 'The First Lady', as they called Robin, ran a very efficient homestead and was the perfect choice.

After hearing the news of the impending visit, I thought, *Aha, this is my chance to get curtains for our house*. I'd been studying interior design in the *House & Garden* and *Women's*

Weekly magazines, and getting ideas on what type of curtains would look best. I had a fair idea of what I wanted.

When I asked Tom about it again, he just mumbled. So on Peter Morris' next visit, I made a point of going to morning smoko to speak with him. I didn't want Tom to hear me.

Smoko finished, everyone went back to work, and Mr Morris and I were left.

'You wanted to talk to me about something, Thea?'

'Yes, Mr Morris. As you know, the governor-general and his party will be staying in our cottage. Although it's very comfortable, unfortunately we have no curtains, which I'm sure they wouldn't appreciate.'

'Well, let us go up to your house and have a look.' Which we did. 'Yes, you are quite right, we must get some curtains made before they arrive.'

'I'm quite happy to make them, Mr Morris. We just need to order some material.' I was thinking that David Jones, Myer and Mark Foy's always had beautiful materials.

'Oh no, I'm sure that the Wave Hill store will have material. Let us pay a visit.'

I was horrified. The old devil, a true Vestey man—he was always worried about the budget.

Jack Niven, the storekeeper, greeted us. And, yes, he had some rolls of dress fabric for the Aboriginal women: brown head cloth, pink head cloth and a nursery pattern on blue seersucker. Jack was on my side and mumbled about the limited amount he had to show us.

'Maybe we could order some material, Mr Morris,' I suggested.

The curtains

But no, Mr Morris wasn't going to spend any more money. Dear Mr Morris! Well! That was all I was going to get. I made the curtains; they served their purpose, but only for the bedrooms. I decided that curtain-less windows looked better in the lounge and dining rooms.

30

Cudge and Jack

Several months later, I flew to Darwin to await the birth of my second child. I left my beautiful fifteen-month-old son, Anthony, in the care of his father and grandmother. My mother-in-law, Mary 'Cudge' Connors, had come to take on the cooking at Wave Hill some weeks before, with her second husband, Jack.

As a young girl in Queensland, Cudge had been a champion Lady Rider, and had ridden for the Duke of Gloucester. By 1964, she'd been in the Territory for nearly thirty years. She was a great cook and a great organiser of the Aboriginal female staff. She and Jack had worked at Mount Bundy Station in the 1950s, which had cattle but mainly wild buffalo. Ralph had gone up to work with them for a few years before he'd come to Wave Hill.

Jack was a bush poet. I've included this poem of his, as it reflects a little of what the old Wave Hill was like.

Wave Hill
Navvies in jodhpurs
Women in trousers
Lubras in jeans and living in houses
Bras on their teats and even wear scanties
Now I'm wondering what else they will wear.

There are boisterous jackaroos laughing and gay,
And some old time ringers with nothing to say
There's all kinds of germs and you should hear them curse
For there's three women here and each one's a nurse.

The governor-general, Lord De L'Isle, arrived for his visit accompanied by a small entourage. His aide-de-camp wasn't very happy with his choice between sleeping in our pantry-cum-storeroom or down at the visitors' quarters with the steel beds and corrugated walls. Good thing Cudge was the cook, so there were no worries about the food, and Robin Hill from Nicholson was an excellent hostess.

Down at the site proposed for the new homestead, the contractor Jack Warner finally drew water after drilling for nine months, and drove at speed to inform everyone of his find. Having heard the news, Lord De L'Isle declared his eagerness to go with the staff to the drill site. Someone decided they'd better have a taste of the water, and of course the honour fell to the special guest. He was handed a pannikin filled with this precious liquid. He took one mouthful and started coughing and spitting it onto the ground. It was salt water!

Poor old Jack Warner: how would he have felt? He'd spent the good part of a year billing Wave Hill for his services. Imagine his distress when the Northern Territory 'Holy Grail'— fresh water—had come to naught. At least we weren't going to live up there with rock gardens and daily visits from the settlement folk.

31

The big wait

Leaving a nursing sister called Kathy Dowman in my place, I flew to Darwin not knowing exactly when my baby was due, but feeling that I only had a few weeks to go. No scans in those days.

I stayed with MaryAnn Napier, whose husband, Dave, was a stock inspector for the Department of Primary Industries, and a great friend of Ralph's. This was my first time meeting MaryAnn, who'd just had a baby of her own. I felt an imposition on the family, but no one else seemed to mind.

Every second day I would go into town from their home at Rapid Creek, on the coastal fringe of Darwin, just to give MaryAnn a break. I'd see a movie or just wander around the shops.

For two nights I stayed at the Darwin Hotel for a catch-up with my sister-in-law Faye, who flew in to Darwin on her way south. Tim and Faye were living in Nigeria at the time, as Tim was working as an aerial surveyor for the Nigerian government.

They were given flights home every six months. Instead of returning to Vancouver where they lived, Faye decided to visit her parents in Newcastle, stopping off in Darwin to see me.

Faye and Tim had been living in Canada and America since the late fifties. They'd met and married in Vancouver, then spent two years in Nigeria. Later Tim worked in Saudi Arabia and Algeria. But America had won their hearts. They lived in Honolulu for several years, moved to Los Angeles, and finally retired to Santa Barbara where their daughter and family now live.

Faye and I had a great time together in the old Darwin. I remember her saying, 'How quaint is Darwin?'

It *was* quaint in those days. Not much more than a frontier town. Not like the mammoth, modern metropolis it became after Cyclone Tracy.

The weeks of my confinement dragged on. I was concerned about who would deliver the baby because of the foetal distress experienced by Anthony. I wanted to be sure I had a good doctor on hand in case of complications, so I booked a private obstetrician who'd been recommended to me.

I missed Ralph and Anthony terribly. Occasionally someone would come up from the stations and we'd meet for coffee in town. When Gus Ringler arrived from Nicholson, he rang me and asked, 'Haven't you had that baby yet? What you need is a couple of strong gins. That will bring you into labour.' At the Old Vic Hotel I had several gin and tonics with Gus, but even that didn't help.

*

On a Friday morning two weeks later, I finally felt something happening. *Hooray! My waters must have broken.*

But it wasn't water—it was blood. *No*, I thought. *What's happening?*

MaryAnn raced me to my obstetrician.

I was shocked when he informed me that I had a placenta praevia, a rare condition meaning that the placenta was coming first through the birth canal. Into hospital I went, where I was commenced on a blood transfusion that continued for two days. The obstetrician waited for me to come into labour. I knew the dangers and couldn't quite understand in my befuddled mind what was happening. I was relying on this obstetrician to do the right thing.

Luckily for my baby, and me, my friend Smiddy had come to Darwin for a holiday with her mother, Dr Saunders, a Macquarie Street gynaecologist. Smiddy was there for me and reported back to her mother on my progress—or lack of—during those two days.

There was no way I could notify Ralph except by telegram. So when the pastoral inspector, Reg Durack, came to visit me, I implored him to ask Tom to send Ralph up to be with me. I needed my husband.

But nothing happened. We sure had to be strong women in those days.

That Saturday Dr Saunders attended a cocktail party at the hospital and met Father John Flynn, the ophthalmologist turned priest who'd married me and Ralph. She expressed her concerns about my confinement to him.

Sunday afternoon found me with nasogastric tube, catheter and intravenous fluids in place, being raced to the theatre. I was thinking, *I wonder if this doctor has ever done a caesarean section.* Was I going to survive? There was nothing I could do, so I shut my eyes and prayed.

I awoke during the night with a ghastly pain where they'd cut me open, so I knew I was still alive.

In the morning they brought in my baby—a gorgeous little boy with a Mr Magoo nose. David had arrived! He was placed in a cot beside my bed. I was so relieved, but so sore.

A little while after my caesar, Smiddy rang the hospital and asked the nurse in the maternity ward, 'Has Penny arrived?'

'Yes,' was the reply, with the nurse thinking Smiddy was just asking if I'd had my baby. My second child was always going to be named either David or Penny.

Smiddy excitedly sent telegrams to Ralph, my mother and Cudge, to announce the arrival of a girl, Penny.

The next day, friends started popping in and saying, 'Congratulations, you've had a girl.'

Defensively I replied, 'No, it's a boy—and his name is David.'

Poor little David. I thought he might hear them and feel unwelcome. At first I couldn't work out why they believed I'd had a girl, but then I received telegrams from Ralph, my mother and Cudge, all welcoming Penny, and I realised Smiddy had told everyone!

Smiddy came back with me to Wave Hill a week after I was discharged from the hospital. Anthony was now seventeen months old, and he didn't know me. It was heartbreaking at first, but he soon came around to accepting me as his mother.

Everyone was busy getting ready for the Negri Races. I was tempted to ask Ralph not to go, but he really had no option: he was in charge of organising everything, especially the horses. Smiddy offered to stay on, but I didn't want her to miss out on the best race meeting ever. Off they all went. Tom and Anne were still on holidays and Reg Durack was sent down to look after Wave.

Anthony, David and I had a very peaceful week, except when 'Mad' Maria, one of the dining-room girls, started terrorising Reg. He asked me to go up to the settlement with him to assess her condition. She was running around, lifting her dress over her head and screaming. The Darwin doctor had seen Maria before and prescribed medication for what would now probably be called bipolar disorder. Taking it with me, I gave her a dose that settled her down. Maria was the only mentally ill patient I had in the north, and her disorder only affected her now and then.

Six weeks after David's birth, I had trouble with my wound. One by one, every stitch site became inflamed, followed by the eruption of a stitch that left a nasty fissure. I had to go on antibiotics that tainted my milk. David refused to drink, which was most distressing. I was a very good 'milker' and wasn't keen on bottle-feeding. Eventually, I had no other option. There was no formula, just powdered milk. The milking cows had gone by this stage; I'm not sure why. I've wondered since if the powdered milk contributed to David having a broken collarbone at eighteen months, a broken arm at two and a half, and a broken leg at seven.

On one of his visits, Father Flynn christened our second son David James Hayes. Len Brodie, a stockman, was the godfather, and Kathy, the nursing sister at the time, stood in as godmother for Smiddy.

Ralph, the boys and I went on holidays a little later, driving to Wollongong to see my family, on to Sydney to socialise with friends, and then to Scarborough, Queensland, to visit Ralph's grandparents, the Taylors. It took around five days to drive south, as it was over three thousand kilometres to Sydney and more to Wollongong. We camped nightly, all in one big swag, always settling on sites hidden away in the bush. I washed the boys' nappies at service stations, then hung them out the car windows, letting the wind do its job, as we sped along. No disposable nappies back then!

If I've been giving you the impression that our camping trips all went smoothly, I apologise. On that trip, one memorable event in Outback Queensland not only threatened to bring our camping days to an end, but us as well!

We set up camp in what we thought was a good spot, with the four of us snuggled in our giant swag. At about three in the morning I woke and let out a scream—I could hear the sound of an approaching train that seemed to threaten to flatten our campsite. We got up and scurried to and fro as the overnight freight train picked up speed, hurtling on towards Brisbane. On closer inspection, it was revealed that a paddock fence separated our campsite from the railway track.

The big wait

It was a most unsettled group of campers who hopped back into the communal swag for four or five hours of fitful sleep before the next leg of the journey began.

32

Back to Gordon Downs

Returning from holidays we were given some great news: Ralph was to be the manager of Gordon Downs Station. We were so pleased, not only about the promotion, but also because life with Tom had become a little difficult.

The water supply for Wave Hill came from a bore and was pumped into an overhead tank. A weight hung on a rope outside the tank with a float inside to show the water level. If the tank was getting empty, the weight would be high, and whenever the weight got high, Tom would start moaning, 'They're using that *thing* again,' referring to our flushing toilet. Much better we go, and he and Anne could move into the cottage where we thought they should have been right from the start.

The Vesteys provided all the furniture on their stations, so we had only our clothes and personal effects to take, including our beautiful Samoyed, Dasher. Little boys need a pet, and when we'd seen Dasher for sale in a pet shop in Woollahra, while on holidays in Sydney, we bought him and he fitted the bill perfectly.

Tom sent a truck over to Gordon with our gear and Dasher. Ralph, the boys and I travelled there in our good old Humber. We were excited at the prospect of taking on our first management job, particularly at such a gorgeous location in the Kimberley.

The Jones family—Stan, Mary and their five children—were eager to leave, so we only had a couple of nights with them, but that was all right. Stan and Mary had managed a very efficient station, and Ralph knew the workings of Gordon Downs, as we'd relieved there the year before. The homestead looked a picture with its perfectly manicured lawns, first-rate vegetable garden and spotless buildings. Morning and afternoon smoko were served on the lawn under a shady tree in the summer and in the sun in the winter.

Of the one hundred or so Aboriginal residents, more than half had jobs around the homestead or in the stock camp. Those not employed came up one day a week to do a job. Some women would scrub baking dishes, bread tins, and pots and pans with sand—very effective in removing gunk. A team of men carried flagstones to build a boundary wall at the back of the station.

Against one wall of the kitchen was a long table where all the Aboriginal staff collected their food. The beef house and the large bread oven, which was encased in ant bed, were just outside the kitchen. When we had a killer, the people from the camp, pensioners and children, would come up to get their share of fresh meat. Our meals were taken down to the homestead from the kitchen and kept warm in a fuel stove, in what we called the pantry.

The downstairs of the two-storey homestead consisted of four rooms: pantry, dining, lounge and recreation. The highly polished floors were made of paint-infused cement. There were three Aboriginal girls working downstairs; each had one room to clean. It would take them half a day to wash the floors and wipe over every bit of furniture. I thought this was overdoing it, but Ralph said, 'Why change when they're in a routine and happy with it?'

Above the dining-room table was the 'punkah', a type of fan that originated in India. It consisted of a few flaps of leather hanging from a wooden frame. A rope connected one end to the other, and extended about two metres to the 'punkah puller', an employee who would sit on the floor and pull the rope backwards and forwards, creating a cool breeze around the table. One of the house girls, Dora, was the punkah puller. It was her special job; her husband, Paddy, was always keen to do it, but only when she allowed him. He pulled with the rope around his toe. Quite often my little boys would sit on their laps and help pull. Our quarters and visitors' rooms were upstairs. The infamous Greek boys had worked for Stan Jones and constructed magnificent floor-to-ceiling varnished wooden cupboards in the dressing room. When the old kitchen had burnt down some years earlier, Stan had employed them to erect a platform on four pillars with an entrance from the upstairs verandah. It was known as the Launching Pad. Underneath was a sandpit for the children. They played in it for hours, driving their little trucks and bulldozers, and swearing as they'd heard the men do in the stockyards—much to their mother's horror.

On very hot nights, the Launching Pad was the ideal place to sit and have an evening drink, or to sleep on steel folding beds that we kept handy. One night several years later, we decided to sleep out as it was oppressively hot. Ralph was inside doing some paperwork. I was reading in my bed on the Launching Pad and the boys were jumping up and down on mattresses.

I felt the whole Pad suddenly start to shake.

Earthquake! Grab the children! How can I grab three children at once?!

Pictures came vividly to my mind of this monolith collapsing with us on top.

Abruptly, it was over and all was still.

I raced in to tell Ralph of our horrible experience, but he'd felt nothing. The following morning we heard on the radio that the town of Merredin in Western Australia, over three thousand kilometres away, had experienced a magnitude 6.5 earthquake, and tremors from a northern fault line had been felt all the way to the Kimberley.

Ralph took much pride in anything he did. He was highly conscientious and an excellent manager, and had a wonderful knack of being able to work men very well. The Aboriginal residents all loved him. He spoke to them in their language, which he learnt rapidly.

Aside from us, the white staff at Gordon Downs were two jackaroos, Colin and Mike, and a bore mechanic, Des Peterson. The bookkeeper/storekeeper, Des O'Donahue, and his wife,

Dulcie, lived in a cottage next door to our house and looked after themselves.

Having taken on Gordon Downs, we'd also taken on the care of Janice, a lovely half-caste girl who had been brought out of the camp by Stan and Mary some years before. Janice lived in the homestead and spent every school term in Derby, seven hundred kilometres away on the West Australian coast. Derby is a cattle-shipping port where the jetties are ten metres high due to tide rises; there are mudflats, crocodiles and mosquitoes in abundance. After her schooling, Janice married Des Peterson, and now lives in the small town of Fitzroy Crossing.

At the beginning of each school term, Father Maguire, the Balgo mission administrator, would drive from Balgo—approximately 250 kilometres north—to the station to pick up Aboriginal children aged between nine and fifteen; there would have been fifteen to twenty of them. They went to school at Balgo for the whole term. More than two hundred Aboriginal people had come in from the Great Sandy Desert to live in this Catholic mission, established in 1939.

Our dear friends Nora and John Kirsh, whom we met when they came to Balgo, gave two years as volunteers to assist Father Maguire. They returned to Balgo Mission for another five years—John taking on the job of cattle manager—and then they and their nine children ended up on their own property in Queensland.

Father Maguire always arrived at Gordon Downs with a bottle of Scotch, which he loved—and we loved listening to his yarns.

After a day or two at the station, he'd take the children back to Balgo. The kids looked forward to returning to school with Father. The parents didn't seem to mind, either!

Father Maguire had been brought up on a dairy farm in Victoria; he joined the army until he was kicked out for causing a strike over poor-quality food. He then became a priest, doing his studies in Rome. He loved horses and used well-known sires to breed his own thoroughbreds.

When the 'walkabout' disease affected many stations in the area, Father Maguire supplied Kimberley stations with Balgo-bred horses. Walkabout or Kimberley horse disease affects horses that graze on the genus *Crotalaria*, commonly known as rattlepods. The plant contains poisonous substances that damage the liver. Affected horses appear to be blind and wander aimlessly, bumping into objects, hence the name 'walkabout'. They rarely survive this debilitating disease.

33

Me Missus Cook

Eager to improve my culinary skills, and not very impressed with our station cook, I told Ralph my intention of doing the cooking myself. 'Managers' wives have never been allowed to cook on the stations,' he replied.

What a lot of hogwash, I thought, so I wrote to Peter Morris. I stated that I wished to cook for my family, and that to cook for three others—the bore mechanic and two jackaroos—would be a delight. Hence, I got the job of cook at Gordon Downs

My cooking bible was still *Mrs Beeton's*, although the last time I'd used it extensively was when Ralph and I were first married. Inexperience and fancy recipes didn't mix. 'Please, can we just have plain steak?' he would beseech me. I decided I was going to become a first-rate cook at Gordon Downs, but still to this day haven't got there.

Three girls worked in the kitchen; Topsy cooked the corn beef, Polly did the washing up and Tamarin cooked the bread. My mother-in-law, Cudge, had given me some advice: 'Never learn to make bread.' Good advice, as we needed ten loaves a day at Gordon to feed the troops, and Tamarin did a great job.

Topsy was the best corn beef cook *ever*, especially of brisket. Under a large mulga tree not far from the kitchen, a pot of boiling water sat over a campfire. The salted beef would be taken from the meat house, rinsed off, and thrown into the water with a handful of 'Quickqurit', a curing salt which puts the pink colour into the beef. The meat simmered until tender, was tested with a fork and then pulled out, ready to taste. It would literally melt in your mouth. Delicious!

My lunch menu always included corn beef, thus several frequent visitors referred to me as the 'Corn Beef Queen'. I used to think that if I ever moved back to Sydney, I'd open a cafe near David Jones in Market Street and serve fresh corn beef, on fresh crusty bread, with a dill pickle on the side. I would make a fortune.

While I was busy cooking, my house girls, Sarah and Larrikin, would wash and dress my children, take them down to the dining room for meals and play with them, but Ralph or I was always there when they went swimming.

The boys learnt to swim at Gordon in a 4000-litre, cement-lined tank behind the vegetable garden. It was a little over a metre deep, so my little boys had to hang on to the sides until they learnt to keep themselves afloat. We'd go out swimming nearly every day in the hot weather.

The furniture upstairs in our private lounge room was fairly limited, so Ralph and Des Peterson set out to make a couple of lounge chairs of welded steel and timber. I requested flat wooden arms to put an ashtray on, as we all smoked in those days. The result was two very comfortable chairs in our lounge.

Des and Ralph also made a cart for Dasher to pull, although sometimes Ralph would bring up one of the goats to pull it instead. I'd get in with the children on those occasions, just in case they went too fast, but the faster the better as far as the boys were concerned—they loved it!

34

Opening night in London's West End?

Many people who came to Vestey properties were guests of the company. One was Keith Michell, the Shakespearian actor, film star and artist. He visited Wave Hill and was then given a lift to Gordon Downs by Graham Johnson, the droving overseer, who brought him in his truck.

When they were about halfway, Keith said, 'Excuse me, old chap, do you mind if I sit on the back? I wouldn't mind getting a suntan while I'm here.' To protect his lips he covered them with lipstick—well, he's an actor after all.

Who should come along but Graham Fulcher, whom I'd met at my first Negri with his then fiancée, Robyn. He was on his way to Wave Hill from Kirkimbie Station, which he and Robyn were now managing.

'Where's this famous film star?' bellowed Graham Fulcher peering into the front of the vehicle.

Just then this apparition, stripped to the waist, jumped up from the back of the truck where he'd been lying on a towel. They greeted one another cordially then Keith made himself comfortable again reclining in the sun.

At Gordon Downs, Keith enjoyed every aspect of the station. He went out to the stock camp to meet and observe the Aboriginals and had long discussions with Ralph about their culture.

Keith is an artist and drew excellent sketches of us all, calling Ralph's portrait *The Missing Link*. He also decided to write a play based on Aboriginal people in the Outback. Ralph, with his vast knowledge of Aboriginal culture and his ability to understand many of their languages, was appointed as Keith's chief adviser. Keith and Ralph spent many hours discussing various aspects of this play. We were told that should it be a success, Ralph and I would be flying from Australia to London's West End to attend opening night.

Wow! That sounded exciting. What would we wear? Where would we stay—the Dorchester, the Savoy or the Ritz? Who would we meet?

Keith stayed for about ten days, and we did hear from him several times after he returned to London, but never about the play. However, an invitation arrived for Keith's art exhibition, in which he had paintings of a corroboree performed by the Aboriginal people who lived at Gordon Downs.

Did we think of going? No, not really. It was a busy time for us in the middle of the dry season, and we were expecting our third child, so it could have been a little difficult. But Keith's whole visit had been a lot of fun, especially when we'd been thinking about that opening night. It was a thrill to receive the invitation.

35

Halls Creek

Everyone knew everyone in the Outback—if you hadn't met someone, you'd hear all about them and eventually meet.

In 1965, an invitation came to Gordon Downs asking me and Ralph to attend the wedding of Tom Quilty's son Basil to Leslie Elliot, a Sydney girl who was the governess at Inverway Station, neighbouring Wave Hill.

Tom, a pioneering pastoralist, poet and outstanding cattleman, together with his wife, Olive, lived at Springvale Station. The annual Tom Quilty Gold Cup Endurance Ride was instigated by R.M. Williams after Tom donated a gold cup as a perpetual trophy; this ride is considered the pinnacle of endurance riding in Australia. The whole Quilty family had properties in the Kimberley: Mick and Edna on Landsdowne, Cherry and Mick on Ruby Plains, and soon-to-be-wed Basil and Leslie on Bedford Downs, out of Halls Creek. The ceremony was to be held at Hall's Creek, 130 kilometres from us over a pretty rough road.

I was about twenty-eight weeks pregnant with my third child and really starting to show, so I made a dress of white linen with tucks down the front to disguise the tummy. As wigs were in that year, a black bouffant hairdo completed my outfit.

The wedding took place in the beer garden of the hotel where we stayed, and the reception was at the Halls Creek town hall. A great time was had by all. Tom Quilty played the saw in the beer garden: the handle between his legs, the far end held with one hand, and his other hand drawing a bow across the back edge of the tool. It was pretty scratchy, but clever nonetheless.

My brother-in-law Lynn Hayes ran around doing a survey, asking all the young ladies if women farted just like men. Cheeky devil!

But by the third day I was anxious to get home, as I wasn't feeling terribly well. On arriving back at the station, I called Sarah and Larrikin to bathe and feed Anthony and David while I went to bed. I started having abdominal pain and felt mildly nauseated. *I must have overdone it*, I thought. *How stupid I was to have gone to the wedding. Too late now!*

In the meantime, Ralph presumed I was going into labour and sent Popeye the gardener down to the camp to warn the Aboriginal midwives, who probably came up to the homestead and sat around having a chat in the laundry, waiting for further directions from Boss Ralph. He kept tiptoeing into our bedroom and whispering, 'You all right? How're the tummy pains?'

I had no idea that he was agonising over a possible delivery, because I knew I wasn't in labour. Poor guy!

The following morning, gazing into the mirror, I was shocked to see dull yellow eyes looking back at me. My urine had turned bright yellow. I knew then that I had hepatitis, a very contagious disease affecting the liver that causes jaundice, nausea, extreme fatigue and abdominal pain—and, in pregnancy, can lead to early delivery. One of the stockmen on Rosewood Station had contracted the disease some time ago. A month ago Ralph hadn't been very well; I think he may have had it too, and that's probably how I picked it up.

As I hadn't gone into labour, earlier that morning Ralph had decided to make a quick trip out to the stock camp. I sent a note over with one of my house girls to Des O'Donaghue, the bookkeeper/storekeeper, and asked him to contact the Royal Flying Doctor with all my signs and symptoms. Des quickly contacted the flying doctor base in Wyndham and a plane was dispatched immediately.

'Sarah, Larrikin,' I said, 'you fella look after dat Anthony and Harji—' a nickname that Anthony at the age of two had given David as a baby '—till Boss Ralph get back. Me gotta go hospital.'

The hospital admitted me because of the risk of going into early labour, or so the doctor informed me when I reached Wyndham. Being infectious I had a room to myself. Meals were brought in, but no one wanted to take the trays away. I ended up with half the hospital's crockery and cutlery! They kept me in hospital for a week, but I was feeling better and bored after one day.

However, I felt incredibly weak once I returned home on the mail plane. I had to rely on my faithful house girls to look after the boys and the kitchen girls to do all the cooking. I'd wander up to the kitchen each morning to go through the menu for the day—then, exhausted, head back to bed. It took a few weeks before I was really well again. The girls were marvellous.

36

Number three arrives

Having had so much trouble when David was born, I decided to go back to Crown Street Hospital and book Dr John MacBeth again for my third delivery.

At thirty-two weeks I was ready to leave for Sydney. Ralph drove me in our Humber Super Snipe to Darwin Airport, while Gus and Pat Ringler looked after the boys. On the way home Ralph was about twenty kilometres from Nicholson Station when he noticed the temperature gauge high and smoke pouring from the engine. He just had time to jump out before the whole car burst into flames.

Gus was starting to become concerned as to where Ralph had got to, because a message had come through on the radio from Wave Hill that he was leaving for Nicholson at 9 a.m. It was well into the afternoon and there was still no sign of him. Gus drove out on the road to Wave, only to find a miserable sight: Ralph sitting sadly beside the burnt-out remains of the his beloved Humber.

Number three arrives

Everyone surmised that Ralph had put a match to it for the insurance. He hadn't, of course, but they liked to have a bit of fun and tease him about it. The site, near Yellow Waterhole, was later called 'Ralph's Folly'.

After spending a few weeks with my mother in Wollongong, I went to Sydney to stay with my old overseas mates Jill Askew and Jennifer Fisher. I felt single again—except for a big bump! I loved going to opening nights of art exhibitions, seeing many plays and films, and dining out at delightful restaurants.

Jason William Hayes was born on 21 July by caesarean section—a beautiful healthy baby. After Jason's delivery I went to stay with my mother again, and three weeks later I was ready to return to Gordon Downs. But before I could make a booking, a telegram arrived from Ralph:

> *Don't return yet. Epidemic of gastro-enteritis in the Aboriginal camp. Babies have died.*

I wasn't so worried about my two older boys: they were three-and-a-half and two years of age, and being strong, healthy children were not as susceptible to gastro as newborn babies. I knew they were in safe hands with Ralph and my faithful house girls.

After waiting a few more weeks, I finally flew in to Gordon Downs with baby Jason. Ralph and the boys were besotted with him. We felt very blessed to have such a healthy child, especially when the three sick babies from the Aboriginal camp had died in Wyndham.

The same week that I arrived back, the flying doctor flew in to our airstrip to return the three bereaved mothers. As soon as the plane landed, the women disembarked, raced over to the edge of the airstrip and proceeded to repeatedly bash their heads with rocks, which is their way of grieving for a loved one. Blood was spurting everywhere. Ralph sent the women back on the same plane to Wyndham for treatment.

The terrible gastro infection struck the nursing sister's baby at the Halls Creek hospital. The baby didn't survive the flight to Derby. We felt so lucky to have a healthy baby, and so sorry for those devastated mothers.

I asked Popeye if he would make me a coolamon for Jason: a shallow wooden dish with curved sides, like a miniature canoe, a coolamon is used by Aboriginal women to carry fruit and nuts, as well as to cradle babies. Popeye did so, and I carried Jason around in it for quite some months; it was much cooler for the baby than being carried on my hip.

Popeye also made a boomerang; a nulla-nulla, a heavy, carved hunting stick about a metre long; and a shield made of balsa wood with a depressed handle. All were painted with dots: red and white ones from the Vestey paint. I still have these precious artefacts today.

We had a christening party for Jason. The priest came down from Wyndham, as that was our diocese in Western Australia. Heather and Rod Russell, the couple who'd married just before us, were now managing Sturt Creek about ninety kilometres south of us. I asked Heather and Milton—Ralph's brother, who was visiting at the time—to be Jason's godparents. Milton had come north for Lynn's upcoming wedding to Patsy Collins, Anna and Cowboy's daughter from Uralla Station near Wave; the wedding was to be in Katherine.

We didn't have a Negri race meeting for a few years, as the government resumed Ord River Station. The Ord produced the tenth-largest volume of water of any river in the world. It was resumed as part of an irrigation scheme built in stages during the twentieth century, producing Australia's largest artificial lake.

There was a risk of vast amounts of silt pouring into the dam from the lower reaches of the river near the cattle station, so the government paid for fencing, ploughed up over 40,000 hectares and planted buffel grass before the station was closed down. All the cattle were sold or sent to other Vestey stations.

A new Negri racecourse was being organised on Nicholson Station, but that would take a few years to complete, so we all went to the Halls Creek Races. Our camp was set up on the outskirts of town, and it wasn't quite as luxurious as our last Wave Hill camp at Negri had been. Of course, being in a town we didn't have to bring too much food, and could always get ice for the cold beer.

My friend Smiddy flew up via Perth and arrived in the middle of the night, having somehow procured a lift from Derby on a road train. Lots of friends were there for the one day of races and one day of rodeo. We didn't do well with our racehorses that year, but we had a great time.

37

Drought and flooding rains

Months later, Ralph contacted Milton, who was working in New South Wales, and offered him the position of head stockman at Gordon Downs. Milton accepted and took over the running of the one and only stock camp at Gordon.

When he first arrived we were still in drought: it hadn't rained in three years.

Because the artesian bore provided plenty of water for the homestead, we didn't notice the lack of rain. The lawns always looked green; the vegetables, flowers and shrubs were watered. Out on the black soil plains it was a different story. With hardly any feed for the cattle, many were sent off to Vestey stations in the Territory. At least we didn't have cattle dying everywhere.

Occasionally we'd look to the sky, see dark, threatening clouds, and think, *We're finally going to have a storm*. The girls would rush around pulling the canvas blinds down on all the gauzed, glassless windows. Upstairs in the bedrooms, the windows had tin louvres that provided some protection. But all we received was excessive wind, tons of dust and a very thin layer of mud.

Then, early in 1966, it really started to rain. We were actually in the eye of a cyclone that had settled over Gordon. It rained for seven days: 450 millimetres in total. It was wonderful! Our boys were so excited—we all ran out in the rain, jumping up and down and screaming with joy. We were so thankful.

The chook and goat yards were flooded, so my dear brother-in-law Milton brought half-drowned chickens and goat kids up to the kitchen. They were put into the men's dining room, beside the kitchen where the fridges were kept. Staff never used it, but the chooks and goats were well accommodated. Meanwhile, the laundry girls brought all the wet washing over to the kitchen; linen was draped across chairs everywhere. I was trying to cook and look after the flood victims as well, until Ralph decided Milton could give the chef a break.

How happy was I! I left the cooking up to Milton and disappeared into the house to catch up with other chores, have more time with my children and get into that special book I was dying to read. Milton was a good cook and got on really well with the girls, so everyone was happy. Especially me.

Just after it stopped raining, a RAAF Iroquois helicopter was sent from Wyndham to search for a missing stockman on Gordon Downs. He wasn't one of ours. He'd been driving through when the cyclone hit and was marooned by floodwaters. They did find him but he wanted to stay with his vehicle until the road dried out. After giving him some rations, the chopper dropped in to Gordon to let us know the situation. They told us that there was a continuous stretch of water from Wyndham to Gordon: that's an expanse of about 1600 kilometres.

Channels of water were running down the hill in front of the house, turning and continuing down the road towards the Aboriginal camp, which luckily was on higher ground.

And what was Dasher doing? Chasing and barking at the rushing water. There were hundreds of fingerlings, all swimming down the stream. Dasher chased them for days. To get some peace and to give him a rest, we had to chain him up.

Where had they all come from? Fish eggs are laid and, as the water dries up, they fall down cracks or are covered with mud and dust. When the big rains come during a good wet season, which should be annually, the eggs hatch and swiftly grow to adult size, five to six centimetres in length. They swim up any moving water, mate and again leave millions of eggs to survive until the next big rain. I'm sure it rained fish one year at Wave Hill, as we found fingerlings on the tennis court and lawn after one storm, and there was no running stream to bring them there.

In June 1967, a journalist from the *Territorian* newspaper in Darwin came to do a story on properties in the East Kimberley area, following the wonderful rains. The headline read: 'The Kimberley's King Size Season'.

The Kimberley has some of the finest cattle country in the world but up until then had been subjected to a series of bad patches. For three years in a row no rain fell, or very little. The next two seasons produced widespread and steady rains.

The response of the country and the cattle was remarkable. In fact, it was hard to look back and believe that a drought had persisted for so long. Fat cattle stood knee-deep in oceans of Mitchell and Flinders grasses. The billabongs were brimming and the creeks and rivers flowing fast.

Truly a land of drought and flooding rain.

38

The Wave Hill Walk-off

1966

One morning in August 1966, when we were having smoko on the lawn at Gordon Downs, a vehicle turned up in the driveway. It was Gus Ringler, who'd just driven from his home at Nicholson. The 'grapevine' was our source of news from the other stations, and our main bringer of information was Gus. As the improvement overseer, he frequently visited all the Vestey stations. We would hear about the new nursing sister at Wave Hill, or that there was a new manager at Kirkimbie, or who'd moved to what station. Gus was a mine of information.

After he'd been warmly welcomed by all the staff, Ralph inquired, 'What's been happening in the country?'

'You won't believe this,' Gus said. 'The Aborigines have walked off Wave Hill and gone on strike. Of the 240 Aborigines on the station, only three remain.'

We were flabbergasted. We'd left Wave only twenty months before. Everyone had seemed happy. There were no complaints about conditions; the Aboriginal employees and their families in the camp were fed and clothed. Their health was always a priority, with a nursing sister there at all times. However, it was the wage issue that was the big concern. Wages paid to employees, both white and Aboriginal, were set by the Pastoral Workers Award.

As far as I know, the rate for an Aboriginal man was $6.82 per week plus keep for himself, a wife and one child; the total keep for the family group was assessed at about $14 per week. A white stockman's wage was $23 per week plus keep. By my calculations, with 140 family members residing in the camp, the one hundred adult Aboriginal workers were supporting 1.4 family members each, plus themselves, with food, clothing, accommodation and health care. All but the health care was provided by the Vesteys.

After the walk-off there was much publicity in all the newspapers, blaming the pastoralists for failing to meet their responsibilities as employers. They were expected to do the government's welfare work—to play a 'paternalistic' role. Government programs for Aboriginal people in the Territory were shockingly inadequate in their enforcement. They just didn't seem to have an answer for the assimilation of the most neglected minority in our Australian culture.

The head of the Gurindji tribe, Vincent Lingiari, had broken his leg in the stock camp in 1965 and was flown to Darwin Hospital. There Dexter Daniels, the Aboriginal organiser for the

Northern Australian Workers' Union, together with Frank Hardy, a non-Aboriginal novelist and political activist, had visited him.

At the Native Wage Case in 1966, before the full bench of the Arbitration Commission, the pastoralists and Peter Morris proposed new rates of pay for workers, stressing that while these were still low, full wages for all Aboriginal people would see a reduction of at least 50 to 80 per cent in Aboriginal employment, as well as a major disruption to their way of life.

According to Mr Morris, at a lecture he gave to the Australian History section of the Wonthaggi University of the Third Age in September 2006: 'I do remember that throughout the Native Wage Case, the unions did not produce one Aboriginal witness. I believe this was because it wasn't the Aborigines pushing for the wage claims.'

In March 1966, the Commission decided to delay until 1968 the payment of award wages to male Aboriginal workers in the cattle industry.

On 23 August 1966, after he returned to the station, Vincent led his people—the stockmen, the gardeners, the house girls, the pensioners and the children—on a thirteen-kilometre walk to Wattie Creek. This was a sacred place of spiritual significance— and that's all it had to offer these people, who named their new community Daguragu. Not only did the Aboriginal employees lose their jobs, but they also had to move off their country and away from the parental supervision of the station management.

Historians and witnesses have long debated the facts of the Wave Hill Walk-off; one supposed fact is that the Aboriginal people were only given bones and offal from the killer for food. My memory is that every week we had three killers at the homestead and one in each of the stock camps: seven killers for the whole station, among 270 people. That's four kilograms of meat per person per week.

All the workers were fed; they had beef and bread, tea and sugar. They didn't like vegetables, or milk in their tea. Houses were built for them but they found them too hot, as we did in our quarters, and if someone died in one of the houses the Aboriginal employees never went back inside. Every wet season they would go walkabout for a couple of months and on their return were always eager to get back to their duties. They'd seemed proud of their jobs and contented in their situation.

The strike went on for years. It was well supported and made headlines around Australia. The focus of the campaign soon spread to include issues about ownership of traditional land. The Wave Hill Walk-off became the first claim for traditional land in Australia.

Gurindji Blues
By Ted Egan

Poor bugger me, Gurindji
Me bin sit down this country
Long time before Lord Vestey
All about land belongin' to we
Oh poor bugger me, Gurindji

Outback Nurse

Poor bugger me, Gurindji,
Man called Vincent Lingiari
Talk long all about Gurindji
'Daguragu place for we
Home for us Gurindji'
But poor bugger blackfeller, Gurindji

39

Months of measles

In late November, our stock camp was dismantled for the year. All the staff went on holidays. Ralph and I were looking forward to a lovely quiet family Christmas at Gordon Downs. However, over the next two months the whole Aboriginal camp—men, women and children—went down with the measles. Not all at once, just a few cases every couple of days.

An infectious and virus-borne disease, measles affects the respiratory system. Symptoms are fever, cough, runny nose, red eyes and a generalised skin rash all over. There are some quite nasty complications: pneumonia, otitis media (middle ear infection) and acute encephalitis (inflammation of the brain).

My patients arrived at the homestead flushed with high temperatures, their eyes watery, saying, 'Me proper sick, Missus.' I needed them nearby so I could monitor their conditions; and as the storekeepers Des and Dulcie were away on holidays, I made their lawn the isolation ward.

Twice a day I would take temperatures. If it was elevated, the family would give the patient a shower with the hose, under my instruction; and when the patient was afebrile, I would give them two Panadol. Often if you give paracetamol to a patient with a temperature, it will make them vomit.

The epidemic started in early December and finished at the beginning of February when our little boys went down with this awful disease. Thankfully, everyone recovered without complications.

There have been many changes since 1902, when Mrs Aeneas Gunn wrote *We of the Never Never* on Elsey Station, 115 kilometres east of Katherine. It was now possible to raise a family in the bush without fear of sickness. However, the health of everyone on the stations still depended on the manager's wife, nursing sister or not.

Every morning after smoko, anyone with a medical problem came up to the homestead to see the missus. In the large pantry—where food was kept warm before dinner—was the medicine cupboard, stocked by the Flying Doctor Service when it came every month.

After visits by the eye specialists, who came up either from Sydney or Perth via Wyndham, I instilled eye drops twice a day for a fortnight to every child to treat trachoma. Just like at Wave Hill, everyone had to be inoculated for TB, and given Sabin for polio, plus triple antigen, the vaccine for tetanus, diphtheria and whooping cough. The Royal Flying Doctor from Wyndham picked up any medical emergencies.

Tiger, the bore mechanic's offsider, was struck by lightning during a violent storm when travelling on the back of a truck. Milton said, aghast, 'He's bloody turned white!' He *had* turned white all right, but he was back to his original colour by the time he returned from Wyndham Hospital. He had a few weeks off and then happily went back to work.

In 1966 a medical team from Darwin turned up to examine all the Aboriginal residents for Hansen's disease, more commonly known as leprosy. They took a scraping from the ear of each person. Several weeks later we received a telegram from the flying doctor telling us to have Charlie, our Aboriginal chief dairyman, ready the next day for evacuation—much to our consternation, we were informed that he had 'infectious leprosy'! He was the only person with this disease at Gordon Downs. Ralph, Milton and I drove him out to the airstrip.

Leprosy has affected humanity for thousands of years. Caused by bacteria, it creates dry lesions randomly on the body. When these become infected, fingers and toes can shorten and deform—*not* fall off as we all thought. Most leprosy colonies have closed down, as it can be cured with medication these days. But there are still colonies in India, China and Africa.

We were extremely anxious because Charlie was in charge of milking the cows every day. He'd bring two buckets of milk up to the kitchen, where one was boiled and the other put unboiled into the separator and turned into cream. This was the area of concern: the unboiled milk could have carried the bacteria.

The sister on the plane said, 'One can only be infected with Hansen's disease by very close contact.'

This explanation didn't allay our fears. But time goes on and you stop thinking the worst. Charlie would have been sent to a leprosy colony, but I don't know what happened to him after that.

Another medical situation that was most unusual began one morning when Old Sammy, a relieving vegetable gardener, didn't turn up for work. When we questioned Rosie, his daughter, she told us, 'Dat Sammy, him bin sung.'

She meant that members of the tribe had pointed the bone at him. This was a type of execution, initiated by the tribal leaders for whatever reason. One has to be born into this culture to believe its effects. I found the situation very hard to relate to, but although I offered Old Sammy's family extra food to give him, he refused to eat or drink, literally wasting away day by day.

In three weeks he was dead.

40

An unwelcome trip

Life continued on as usual at Gordon Downs. Then, one morning, I felt a lump in my breast. I was devastated, but I tried to pretend it wasn't there. *Tomorrow morning it will be gone*, I thought. But it wasn't.

Ralph had gone out to the stock camp early that morning. I'd told him about the lump, and we were planning to discuss it that evening. However, as I was feeling very anxious, I sent a message over to Des the bookkeeper with one of the house girls, asking him to please contact the flying doctor asap.

Later that morning a plane flew in to pick me up. Ralph was surprised that I was leaving so quickly, but my policy with any medical problem has always been to see a doctor and get treatment, the sooner the better. The girls, Larrikin and Sarah, were wonderful. They knew how to look after my beautiful boys.

In Wyndham Hospital, after being examined by the doctor, I was back in a plane and heading for Derby to see a surgeon. The hospital was quite modern, thankfully. My surgeon,

Lawson Holmes, was brilliant with a great sense of humour, often cracking jokes and full of fun.

Like many young women, I'd recently discovered the Pill. I was happy with my three children and didn't plan on having more at that stage. Unfortunately, Dr Holmes explained, the hormones in the Pill could be the cause of my lump. 'Now, don't you worry,' he added, 'I'm sure after you have your period, the lump will disappear. In the meantime, as you're a trained nurse, you can help in the Medical Record Department.'

No lying in bed feeling sorry for myself: after breakfast I was off to work. Four days later, my period started, but the lump remained. I was taken to the theatre. The lump was removed under general anaesthetic and sent to pathology in Perth.

A few days later, lying on my hospital bed, I had a visit from Dr Holmes, and this time he looked unusually gloomy. 'The results have come back for half of the tests and they're okay,' he said, 'but the rest have to be done again.'

'What does that mean?' I asked.

'We'll just have to wait and see.'

I couldn't sleep; I worried about leaving my boys motherless.

The next day on his rounds, Dr Holmes—maybe guessing my anxiety—ordered me, with a flourish of his hand, to work in Central Dressings. 'Off you go,' he said, implying no nonsense. This was the department where all the instruments, trays and dressing packs were sterilised.

More days of waiting passed by. Then one afternoon I saw Dr Holmes strolling past the window of Central Dressings, and I know that he saw me. He rang a few minutes later. 'I've just received the results of your lumpectomy,' he said, 'and everything is fine.'

Being paranoid, I thought, *Why couldn't he have told me that when he saw me? Is it really true? Or was the lump cancerous and he doesn't want to tell me?*

Up to his surgery I marched. I knocked on the door and walked in.

'Dr Holmes, I want you to look me in the eye and tell me the truth.'

He just laughed. Everything *was* fine—such a relief.

Some years later, Dr Lawson Holmes was appointed as Director of Health in Western Australia.

I never took the Pill again and fortunately the condition I suffered from does not predispose to cancer. How lucky am I?

41

Romance comes to Gordon

The Negri race meetings were now held several kilometres from Nicholson, and our dongas were now clothed in hessian instead of bushes. All the stations endeavoured to build the most efficient bush camp. This was much easier now being much closer at Gordon Downs, rather than Wave Hill.

It was at the 1966 meeting that Milton met two attractive young women, Madeline and Elspeth, who were travelling around Australia.

'Do you mind if the girls come and stay at Gordon Downs for a while?' Milton asked me and Ralph.

'Of course not, we'd love to host them,' we replied.

I was always grateful for female company. The girls stayed for a couple of weeks before taking off for Queensland. They promised to catch up with us in New South Wales at the end of the year.

On holidays in Sydney the following December, we had a call from Madeline and Elspeth. We made a date to meet at

Taronga Park Zoo. While we were there, I happened to mention that I was about to advertise in *The Sydney Morning Herald* for a governess for Anthony, and I was dreading having to do the interviews.

Madeline excitedly said, 'Please, Thea, can I be the governess?'

I was thrilled to have a delightful girl like Madeline coming as governess: a registered nurse and no interviewing. Perfect!

As I'd booked Anthony into the Sydney Correspondence School during our stay in the city, by the time Madeline arrived, so had the correspondence lessons.

While I remained in charge of the cooking, Madeline did the teaching in the schoolhouse, where her quarters were. In the afternoons she would give the boys riding lessons.

Ralph and I noticed that Milton was continually coming into the station from the stock camp with all sorts of excuses. Some months later, he and Madeline announced that they were getting married.

Great excitement! We started making plans for the guest list, bridal party and menu, and working out how much grog would be required. The pageboy outfits, bridal gown and bridesmaids' dresses were made by Paula Stafford on the Gold Coast—the maker of the first bikinis in Australia. Patsy Hayes (Lynn's wife), Betty Atkinson and I were bridesmaids. Ralph, Lynn and Sabu were groomsmen, and my sons were pageboys.

Cudge, Madeline and I prepared food for a week beforehand. We had chooks, so there were plenty of eggs. I made 150 small pavlovas—one per guest—that melted because I didn't have enough sugar in them; you need plenty of sugar for firmness. I had to do the lot again! By this time I was a pavlova specialist.

There was no running to the local delicatessen; everything we were to serve came from the station—roast beef, steak, sucking pig (we ran our own pigs in a pigsty) and roast chicken, and I think we might have killed a young goat, of which there were about twenty. Plus we had an assortment of salads from the garden. The drinks, of course, came from Halls Creek, more than 150 kilometres away.

Prominent in our minds was that the only road into the station had to cross Sturt Creek. During the long drought the creek had gone dry, but now it was fifty metres wide with only a narrow track of gravel on which to drive. If one of our guests drove off the gravel, the wedding could be delayed or we could have no guests! We asked everyone to arrive early Saturday morning to make sure they all got across well before the wedding, even though it meant putting on lunch.

They came in droves, starting on Friday: the Vestey people, the Underwoods, and friends and family from Halls Creek, Katherine and Brisbane. No one drove off the track and all 150 guests arrived in fine time for the wedding.

The ceremony was held beside a rock pool that we'd created between the kitchen and the homestead. The bride looked beautiful, and it was a stunning service, officiated by the United Church minister from Katherine.

There was tons of food and plenty of grog. Everyone was happy except one guest, Swannie (the jack of all trades from

Wave), who started celebrating before the service and fell asleep on a chair. He woke up an hour later, when photos were being taken of the bridal party, and asked, 'What time's the wedding?'

Beds were allocated to the women, although most people slept in their swags on the lawn. I remember the lounge-room floor being covered in bodies. Many guests made merry until the wee hours of the morning, but Ralph and I had breakfast to think of for 150 people.

While we were all together, we had a Negri committee meeting. Finally, after lunch, the guests started departing. Not all, though—some with no pressing obligations stayed a few more days. The longest-staying guest, of twelve days, was Ralph's dear old Uncle Alec Fraser, who'd been one of 'The Rats of Tobruk'. He was a great character with fascinating stories about World War I.

Uncle Alec, Ralph's grandmother's brother, had become very well known in the seaside town of Caloundra, Queensland, where he'd moored his houseboat on Dicky Beach, an upmarket touristy area. This didn't go down too well with the local council. Many letters of complaint were sent to the editor of the local paper, but Uncle Alec stayed put. How ecstatic Anthony, David and Jason were when I suggested we go and stay the night while on holidays with Uncle Alec in his old, rather fishy-smelling but comfortable bachelor-pad houseboat. Ralph thought I was mad—there was no way that *he* was going to stay in 'the old tub'.

The four of us had a great time when we went to stay: swimming, fishing and watching the passing parade of holiday-makers, who were fascinated by Uncle Alec's home.

There's now a Fraser Park at Dicky Beach named after Uncle Alec.

42

The long weekend

An invitation arrived at Gordon Downs from Jocelyn and Tim Doran, who were now managing Manbulloo Station, requesting the company of Ralph, me, Madeline and Milton at the wedding of Sue and Des, two of their staff, to be held at Manbulloo a few miles out of Katherine. Tim had been a stockman at the Ord River and Kirkimbie stations with Graham and Robyn Fulcher, while Jocelyn had been at school with Robyn. She'd come up to Kirkimbie for a holiday, met Tim and fell in love—another Outback romance.

We left for the wedding early Friday morning. Being a good Vestey manager, very conscious of expenses, Ralph said we would all go in the one vehicle, a Toyota Land Cruiser ute. Great!

Ralph drove. Madeline and her new baby, Danny, sat in the front. My three little boys sat in the back of the utility with Milton and me, plus our luggage and swags. There was no way I was leaving my children in the back without me. We drove to

Wave Hill to pick up Nita Beebe—the partner of Don Hoare, a fencing contractor and yard builder—who was after a lift to Katherine.

At Manbulloo we were accommodated at the homestead, and that night we had Sue's hens' party on the patio near the dining room, while the bucks party for Des was in the old store building. We girls, six of us—including Des's sister, who'd flown up from Perth for the wedding—were drinking and chatting on the patio. Des's sister was very conservative but quite friendly.

We heard a sudden noise and turned to see Graham Fulcher weaving his way towards us. He plonked himself down on a chair in our midst. He then stood and said, 'Greetings, ladies,' and let go with a resounding fart. Not only did he do it once—he did it several times! Robyn and I shrieked with laughter, which didn't impress the Perth visitor at all. She was *not* amused.

In the church the following day, Des's sister sat beside me and Ralph. The organist started playing 'Here Comes the Bride' and everyone turned to look up the aisle. Initially we couldn't see the bride, but Des's sister could, and we knew by her gasp of horror that she didn't approve. Then we saw the bride and knew why: Sue was dressed in a flowing gown of bright-red chiffon, scattered with white spots. The bridesmaids had the white dresses, with red spots. Des hadn't told his sister that Sue had been married before. The poor woman never really recovered from the shock of seeing the bride in red. Of course, today no one would care what colour was worn.

We spent the next morning swimming in the river and lying around on the sandy beach. Unfortunately we had a fright when the Manbulloo bookkeeper drove down the riverbank to the beach and nearly ran over baby Danny, who was asleep in his coolamon.

Ralph then decided we'd better leave. But after we'd picked up Nita in Katherine and driven eighty kilometres, our ute suddenly slowed down and stopped. Nothing could be done. We were wondering what we could do next when we saw a road train coming towards us. It was Jack Beebe, Nita's brother, in a prime mover with triple-trailers behind. He was returning to Katherine after delivering cattle to one of the stations.

Having waved him down and secured his help, Ralph chained our ute to the last trailer and stayed in the driver's seat, while the rest of us climbed into the first trailer, with Madeline and the baby in the cab. We took off. *Wow!* Talk about shocking. Dust and manure were billowing round and round; we had to bury our heads in our laps to breathe. As for poor Ralph, his ute was being thrown from one side of the road to the other. The small mercy was that no vehicles came from the opposite direction.

After a few miles, Jack decided he'd better check on Ralph. This probably saved his life. The Toyota Land Cruiser was left on the side of the road and we all got into our life-saving road train, continuing back to Manbulloo where our beds were waiting for us. Madeline, Nita, the children and I had a sleep while the men picked up and towed the ute back to Manbullo and then had to repair it.

Ralph was so annoyed when he found out what the problem was: someone had tampered with the rotor button while we were packing our gear. We heard later that this person wanted to delay our departure because it would break up the party. We didn't find out who it was, lucky for them!

The men got some sleep before we took off in the Land Cruiser again. After we'd travelled about two hundred kilometres down the Buchanan Highway, Nita cried out, 'My suitcase is missing!' She claimed she'd definitely put it on the ute, so back we went. Eighty kilometres later, there it was on the side of the road.

The next drama was flat tyres when we still had more than 150 kilometres to go to get to Wave Hill. Milton and I walked the few miles to the Top Springs roadhouse. It was nearly midnight and we were thankful when Mrs Hawkes, the proprietor, greeted us warmly, offering rooms for the women and children while the men repaired the punctures.

In the early hours of the morning we took off once again. We finally arrived at Gordon Downs just as the sun came up. There was a buzz of activity and we wondered what was causing the commotion.

We were greeted by Popeye, Larry and all the girls. 'Ralph, Milton, dat bushfire, him been get away, and come this way!'

Sometimes it's great being a woman. The poor guys had to go firefighting for the rest of the day and into the next. Ralph thought that the bushfire must have been caused by a lightning strike.

43

Going back to Wave

Once again it was holiday time, so we did our bi-yearly drive to Wollongong, Sydney and Brisbane. While having dinner with the new Vestey general manager, Roy Bell, and his wife at their home at Mosman, we were told that we were being transferred back to Wave Hill with Ralph as manager, and was that okay? We'd spent five wonderful years at Gordon Downs, but we both felt we were ready for another challenge. So our answer was yes.

Although the Aboriginal people had great respect for Tom Fisher, who'd been managing Wave Hill for twelve years, he'd had no control over the events of the walk-off. They broke his heart, poor fella! Tom and Anne had decided to retire to Kyogle where Tom originally came from.

We went over to Wave Hill for Tom and Anne's farewell party. It was sad to see them leave, but we caught up with them on our next holiday.

*

At Wave we met Gavin MacDonald, who worked as a stock inspector for the Animal Industry Branch run by the Commonwealth government, a department that supervised animal welfare and livestock movements, and collected data such as branding numbers throughout the Territory. Gavin was the stock inspector for fourteen other stations including two Aboriginal communities, and had been based at Wave for a year when we returned.

Pleuropneumonia and brucellosis were diseases prevalent in cattle in the 1950s and '60s. They were tested and treated, and pleuropneumonia has been eradicated up to this point. Cattle ticks were another huge problem with the Shorthorn and Hereford breeds, and plunge dips were the only answer. I found it horrifying to see cattle being shoved into a deep, narrow, long cavern filled with filthy, toxic water, and it was very dangerous for the stockmen too.

The British Shorthorn was the predominant breed in the North back then, some with a mix of Hereford. It wasn't until the seventies that Santa Gertrudis cattle were introduced, and the end of that decade saw the introduction of Brahman, which are not prone to ticks, on virtually every property.

Ralph was thirty-three and represented the new look in cattle management. He'd been bred in the Territory; his father, Dick, had managed the famous Rosewood Station. Working on Wave Hill with great cattlemen like Tom Fisher and Harry Huddleston, Ralph learnt to run a station in a very smooth, efficient manner as was seen in his management of Gordon

Downs. He understood the Aboriginal people and was loved by them, and could speak Gurindji and Warlpiri fluently. With the highly political situation at Wave Hill since the walk-off, Ralph was the perfect choice for manager.

The Vestey Company had decided to rebuild Wave and make it a showplace. We would eventually have a new homestead and buildings at a new site, situated at Number One Bore, thirty kilometres away from the current quarters.

Milton and Madeline were happy to take over the management at Gordon. With their young son, Danny, they needed better accommodation than the quarters they were living in. So our move to Wave worked well for everyone.

I'd received a letter from a fifth-year medical student in Perth, Joanne. She had met someone who'd visited Gordon, and she'd liked the sound of it. She wrote to ask if I needed a governess, as she wanted to have a gap year from her studies. I jumped at the opportunity. Within a few weeks, Joanne arrived on the mail plane, only to be told that we were all about to leave the Kimberley and go to Wave Hill.

Ralph had travelled over the week before on the Gordon truck with most of our gear. In the meantime, Sturt Creek had come up and there was no access by road: the only way out was by plane. The company sent their Cessna from Darwin to collect Joanne, the three boys and me. My sons were delighted about the flight but very sad to leave Gordon Downs, which we all loved.

44

Rat plague and the Hong Kong flu

It felt strange going back to Wave Hill after five years. The old place hadn't improved at all. In fact, it looked messy and unkempt. Thankfully, the old men's quarters beside the overseer's cottage, now known as the manager's house, had been removed.

Don Hoare—the fencing contractor whose partner, Nita, we'd taken to the recent wedding—had set up camp in and around the post office cottage. He thought he was kingpin until Ralph sorted him out. There was also a new bookkeeper, Beryl, a sophisticated Sydney girl who looked completely out of place; an aristocratic Englishman who was supposed to be, but couldn't, cook; and new jackaroos and stockmen. A lot of staff changes in the past five years. And apart from the white staff, we only had a few Aboriginal workers now.

We were extremely busy. I did the nursing and housekeeping. Ralph, in addition to running the station and sorting out his crew, had to monitor work on the new station homestead. He and Gus Ringler, who drove over from Nicholson every week, went out frequently to check on the prefabricated buildings being constructed. The contractors had their own accommodation and cook at the site.

To make our situation even harder, we had a rat plague that had been going on for six months or more. These rats were huge! They ate everything they could find including boots, saddles and bridles. They ran riot in the kitchen. The cook set up a large tub of water with a slippery, fat-laden plank across it and a tasty nibble in the middle; the rats would run across, slip off and drown. Some nights this caught eighty or more in the kitchen alone. And my boys learnt to shoot their slug guns at the rats when they found them in their guinea pig cage.

All the quarters were made of corrugated iron, with an open space about eight inches between the cement floor and the start of the wall. One night Beryl wore an expensive pearl necklace to dinner, as there was a party to farewell one of the staff. Later, when Beryl retired, she left the necklace on her bedside table. In the morning it had gone. She was devastated and went complaining to Ralph that someone had stolen her pearls. Graham MacArthur, a head stockman, was sent to solve the mystery. Looking for clues, he discovered that between the two layers of corrugated iron forming the walls, there was a seven-centimetre gap—and there, sitting on the wooden wall studs, were the pearls.

Our house, being elevated, was the only building that was relatively rat-proof. But even we didn't escape from the wretched things. One evening Ralph and I went to retire and we could hear a rustling and scratching under our bed. 'That's a bloody rat, I'm sure!' Ralph cried. 'Someone must have left the door open.' Dasher was mustered, and he and Ralph—armed with a broom—chased the rat around, over and under the bed, with me standing on the bed screaming. Ralph cursed and Dasher barked. Thankfully, Dasher killed it on the verandah.

In the middle of another night we heard a crunching sound—a rat had chewed halfway through the wooden front door. It was trying to get *out*! Who knows how it got in?

At the height of the plague, a new domestic, Pauline, arrived. When she heard about the rats and saw her room next to Beryl's, she became quite hysterical. 'No, I'm not staying here. I want to fly out—*now!*'

'Sorry, dear,' Pauline was told, 'the next plane doesn't come until next week.'

Fortunately for Pauline, Ralph and I had purchased a caravan on our last holidays. We offered it to her as a rat-free living space.

We'd seen this caravan for sale in Wollongong and thought how wonderful it would be to have on the road rather than camping. We could stop for smoko, lunch, dinner; we had a bed each night. The trouble was that instead of six days travelling back to the station, it took ten as the caravan was heavy to tow. And I wasn't happy when the radiator boiled on the very steep Toowoomba Range and we had to stop. After it cooled down, Ralph said that I'd have to push the caravan to help get it going, which I did, but then I had to run beside the vehicle with my door wide open, Ralph calling, 'Jump in! Jump in!' By this time I was screaming, '*Stop!*' But he couldn't, so I shut my eyes and jumped. Never again! I didn't care much for the caravan after that, but at least it suited Pauline.

The rat plague continued until the CSIRO produced plastic containers that dripped a poisonous liquid, which I think contained warfarin. They were like self-feeders for the rats, and the liquid caused anaemia and a slow death. In the beginning the rats even ate the containers, but gradually, as numbers decreased, they just consumed the poison. Finally they had all gone. The plague at Wave Hill was over after two horrible years.

Joanne lived with us in our house and taught Anthony, then David, with lessons from the Sydney Correspondence School.

Sometime in 1969, the Hong Kong flu arrived. Joanne and I would do the rounds before school commenced each morning. We checked temperatures and gave out paracetamol and cough medicine. I don't think anyone went on antibiotics, but they were there if needed. We would visit the men in the jackaroos' and men's quarters, then see all the sick Aboriginal workers at the hospital, and finally go back to our house where Ralph was ill.

Everyone on the station, even some of our visitors, got the flu, except Joanne, the children and me. Joanne and I were so busy we didn't have time to get sick!

Our house was in a line with the corrugated-iron post office cottage. There was another cottage—where Ces Farrow and his wife had once lived—set between the two. It had been unoccupied for several months.

One day we were having lunch in the main dining room when we heard a great commotion from the Aboriginal workers outside. 'Ralph, fire, quick, dat donga up dere, him go up!'

We all raced out to see what was happening. It was the middle cottage, and it was in flames. Within ten minutes it had burnt to the ground.

Everyone scratched their heads. 'How'd that happen?'

Some thought my boys, playing with matches, might have started it. The comments didn't worry Ralph—but a good thing I didn't hear them.

45

Visitors for Vincent

After the walk-off in 1966, there were only three Aboriginal employees left at Wave Hill, including Brisbane Sambo and Chisel the woodchopper.

With no Aboriginal stockmen, the cattle work had to be done with white contractors. We needed help at the station and in the stock camps, so Ralph went down to Daguragu, the settlement at Wattie Creek, to see Vincent Lingiari and request some Aboriginal staff. Vincent and Ralph had always been great mates. Another friend of Vincent's was also visiting that day, Ted Egan.

Ted sent me this story in an email:

I was at Daguragu in 1969, having a cup of tea with Vincent Lingiari. A little boy called, 'Motor car coming!' Sure enough, a utility arrived. Driving it was Ralph Hayes, manager of Wave Hill Station. The strike was at its peak, and enmities quite strong. I thought, This will be interesting.

Ralph Hayes and Vincent shook hands cordially and exchanged a few words in the Gurindji language. I knew Ralph and shook hands also, but then retired some distance away, as it was none of my business. It was obvious that on a personal level they got on very well, which was not surprising as they both had worked on the station for many years and obviously had high mutual respect. After about five minutes of 'How's your family?' type discussion, Ralph said, 'Old man, I've got a big problem. I've got eight hundred head of cattle on [he named the bore] and the windmill's busted. If I can't move the cattle they're going to perish, but I've got no men.'

Here was the opportunity for Vincent Lingiari to strike a critical blow, but his concern was only for the cattle. He called over to three young fellows: 'You, you, you, go over to the shed and get saddles and bridles. Go with Ralph to move his cattle.'

They did so. Ralph Hayes drove off. I said to Vincent, 'That was interesting.'

He gave a little smile and said, 'Yeah, we gotta look after the white fellas in this country.'

This was in 1969, and a little later one hundred Aboriginal workers—both men and women—were at Wave Hill Station until we left Wave in 1979. This is a little-known fact. They were paid the award wage and were very happy working on the station for Ralph and the Vesteys.

What a great man Vincent was. He had a lot of time for Tom Fisher—in fact, all the Aboriginal employees did. As for Ralph, he and Vincent had a strong affinity for each other. They'd worked and lived together in the stock camp ever since Ralph first arrived in 1955.

In 1959 Ralph had a bad fall from his horse in the stock camp, where he and Vincent were working, and lay semi-conscious on the ground. Vincent cried over him, 'My poor boy, my poor boy!'

46

Making a showpiece

Roy Bell, the new general manager, asked me if I'd like to go to Sydney and buy all the furniture for the new Wave Hill Station. Of course I said yes! I was thrilled. I spent all my spare time studying interior design magazines and taking many trips out to the new station to get measurements. Then I flew down to Sydney.

The Menzies Hotel was fairly new, and that is where I stayed. Every morning the buyer for the Vesteys, Mr Bill Davis, picked me up in a taxi to go shopping. We went to Mark Foy's, Grace Brothers and David Jones. There seemed no limit to what I could spend, as the company now wanted Wave to be a show piece for the Vesteys in the Territory. I was in my element.

The 'in' colours that season were black and orange. I chose black leather lounges and chairs, two orange-and-tan leather reclining chairs, and a beautiful coffee table of varied turquoise-coloured tiles. I also bought a teak bar and stools with orange leather seats, and a dining-room table with twelve chairs matching the stools. To finish the rooms off, we purchased white curtain material with an Egyptian design down the side, plus a couple of wool rugs. I hoped I might be able to buy several paintings to go with the decor, but that was going a little too far with Lord Vestey's money, so I bought them myself and still enjoy them.

Not only did I buy for the homestead, I also had to purchase furniture for the overseer's and mechanic's houses, plus the visitors' quarters.

After a fortnight I was pleased to get home. I was actually sick of luxury accommodation and gourmet food! But of course, it had been a great experience spending money on quality goods with no hesitation, and it was lovely to catch up with my friends.

However, on returning home, I was shocked to hear that Joanne was leaving.

'Thea, I'm sorry,' she told me. 'I wanted to stay till the end of the term, but now feel I can't trust myself.'

Being the only young white woman on the station, Joanne had become very desirable to several of the stockmen. She'd been courted by one in particular, and that was the reason she wanted to leave.

'Well,' I said, 'I'm really sorry too. You've been a wonderful help, but if that's the reason, I think it's probably best you go.'

Joanne went back to her medical studies. I heard she became a well-known anaesthetist in Perth, some years later.

*

Ralph needed a trustworthy overseer, so he rang his good friend Tony Clark, who'd been a head stockman at Wave and best man at our wedding. He was working on a property near Goulburn, but accepted the position. We were so pleased when he and his family—his wife, Sue, and daughters, Bronwyn and Sally—arrived just in time for Christmas.

On Christmas Eve, Don Hoare, a delightful rogue, entertained all of us at a party at his house with his partner, Nita. They put on a very nice meal of roast chicken and vegetables, and I commended them. Next morning there was chaos in our kitchen: the five chickens that had been killed, plucked and put in the fridge the day before were all missing. We knew where they'd gone—eaten last night at Don's dinner party! He wasn't even sorry. Thank goodness we had the Vestey ham, which still came routinely.

Our cook at that time was a well-educated Scottish bloke, John, whose father had given him a one-way ticket to Australia. Although he was a pretty ordinary cook, he was a talented artist. He played the bagpipes and owned a beautiful metre-long English hunting horn, which he sold to me—I have it to this day. He also sold me his painting of a large tree near the creek below the homestead that has my boys' names carved into the trunk.

After Sue and Tony Clark arrived, Sue showed interest in the cooking position. Ralph made John the cook for the Aboriginal kitchen, which was situated behind the store and outbuildings. The Aboriginal staff loved his cooking. But John was asked to leave when Ralph discovered that he'd been using the kitchen as a sly grog shop. He'd buy flagons of wine for two dollars and sell them for five. He had to go and I have no idea what happened to him.

When Ralph replaced John with an Aboriginal cook, the staff bailed up and refused to eat food from one of their own. They had to put up with an Aboriginal cook or go without—they didn't starve. Later we found a suitable cook.

The new station was finished at the beginning of 1970. Sue and Tony were the first to move out, into their overseer's house. Sue took over the cooking in the palatial kitchen. There was a main dining room at one end, then the large kitchen and a huge coolroom, followed by a second dining room for the older white workers, with the cook's quarters at the other end. Everything was stainless steel. They had a mixmaster, toaster, bain-marie and mincer, all modern.

It was the wet season when we all moved from the old to the new Wave Hill. In the wet the staff either went on their bi-yearly holidays or stayed at the homestead where there were heaps of jobs to be completed.

The women supervised their own gardens, often starting with cuttings from their neighbours; these were placed in a bucket of water in a dark spot to shoot. We had an excellent vegetable garden on one side of the house and an orchard on the other. We grew beautiful grapefruit (no sugar needed!), oranges, lemons, grapes and pawpaw. The soil was so rich because our new station was built on the site of an old cattle yard near the bore.

My 'garden boy' was Cudabiddi, a delightful Aboriginal man. He dug the vegetable gardens, I planted the seeds, and he looked after them. He did a wonderful job. The vegetables, grapefruit and oranges were so good that we won many prizes at the Katherine show.

Cudabiddi also trimmed the hedges around the house: not with an electric trimmer but with a pair of shears. They were always perfectly done, flat on top and flat on the sides.

I had great plans for a paved smoko area, which I found in the *Reader's Digest Handyman*, and for a front fence made of two stone walls with a garden in the middle. For this project I was allotted Cudabiddi and Algie, and David Herslett, a stockman. Forty-two years later, David told me that he pulled out from the job because I was being too particular. But I got the front wall and it looked great!

Ralph and I, with help from the gardeners, planted an avenue of poinciana and tulip trees from the entrance of the driveway, down past the cottages to the homestead. Tulip trees are quite large, and native to the United States; their flowers are pale green or yellow and have an orange band at the base. Poinciana grow from five to twelve metres and have a flamboyant display of red flowers. In the house gardens Ralph and I planted several varieties of shrub. Both trees and shrubs were brought all the way from Bundaberg, Queensland.

The Vesteys wanted a show piece and, within a few years, that's what Wave became. You would drive down the gorgeous avenue of trees to a circular driveway in front of the homestead.

Here you could see the lush orchard on the right, and the smoko and barbecue area in front of the dining room.

Within two years all the trees were three metres tall, and red and yellow blooms added to the harmony of the new Wave Hill.

47

Great additions to the station

In Katherine, Sabu married the new Wave Hill nursing sister, Dorothy Dwyer, whom I'd gone to school with in Wollongong. He officially changed his name to Peter David Singh at Dorothy's request, which was very difficult for us to remember as we'd always known him as Sabu. The three Hayes boys were the best man and groomsmen, and Madeline, Patsy and I were the bridesmaids. It was a lovely wedding in the old corrugated Catholic church in Katherine.

Sabu came back to Wave in 1971 as contract musterer and Dorothy did the nursing. Their caravan was parked near the domestic quarters, just opposite the clinic. We three couples— Tony and Sue, Sabu and Dorothy, Ralph and I—had a great social life together: hosting dinner parties, playing records, and dancing to Tom Jones and Engelbert Humperdinck. Dot made delicious Indian curries and we enjoyed many of them sitting out in their marquee beside the caravan.

*

We were pleased to hear in 1972 that Lord Vestey, his cousin Edmund and Edmund's father-in-law were coming for a visit to see the new station. Since my job interview with Mr Alan Perry in 1960, I'd learnt a lot more about the wealthy, aristocratic Vestey family.

Before World War I, the Labor government was looking for a large company interested in producing beef, and willing to take up large tracts of land in the Territory and Kimberley on long leases for minimal rents. The Vesteys accepted and ended up with an area larger than Tasmania.

In 1939, Captain William Howarth Vestey, son of Lord Vestey, Third Lord Baron, married Dame Nellie Melba's granddaughter, Pamela Armstrong. They'd met a few years before in Australia. It was a love match between the granddaughter of the Empire's greatest voice and the grandson of the Empire's greatest fortune. Pamela bore William two sons: Sam in 1941 and Mark in 1943. William was killed in action in 1944. At the age of thirteen, on the death of his grandfather, Sam succeeded as Third Lord Baron.

We found the Vesteys a good company to work for, and very easy to get on with. Sam was a charming, handsome gentleman. He was thrilled with the new station complex, so I suggested the only thing missing was a swimming pool. 'You are so right, Thea,' he said, 'and I'm sure we can do something about that. Ralph, haven't we got a spare water tank?' *Foiled again*, I thought.

But we got our swimming pool in the form of a 40,000-litre corrugated water tank. Thank you, Lord! The whole staff helped in preparing the enormous hole in the ground, lowering the tank into it, sealing, painting, and even building a shade area with seating beside it. Construction took weeks, with the work done mostly on the weekends. And, of course, a pool party followed.

We added chlorine each day and emptied the water out by pump once a month or so, and everyone joined in to clean the pool. Well, not everyone—someone had to hand out the beer. Matt, the mechanic, took on that job.

Sam Vestey only stayed a couple of days. We didn't talk about the walk-off. It was up to him to bring the subject up, and he didn't with me. He might have with Ralph, but we were just employees.

An addition to our new station came from Brisbane.

Milton's telegram read:

I'm taking the truck to Brisbane. Anything I can bring back for you?

'Ralph, here's your chance to buy a pianola,' I said. 'Cudge will find one for you.' Ralph had often talked about Grandma Fraser and the wonderful evenings the family had spent singing around the pianola.

Cudge bought a Beale pianola with one hundred rolls thrown in, and Milton brought it back on the truck. Unfortunately, on the day he arrived at the turn-off to Wave Hill from the Buchanan Highway, we'd had a couple of inches of rain. The dirt road from the highway was slippery and muddy, and halfway in was Five Mile Creek. It was also still raining.

Ralph mustered up everyone he could find to go out to help. They went in four-wheel drives plus the tractor. The pianola was a very beautiful, highly polished timber machine that had to be manoeuvred with kid gloves. How, without causing any damage, they lifted it from the truck to the four-wheel drive, then carried it on the hazardous trip into the station, I will never know.

There was a rush to the homestead; all the girls came up from the camp when word got around. Everyone wanted to see this wondrous thing that Ralph had bought. We had the perfect place for the pianola, just inside the double doors of the lounge room. Everyone tried to squeeze in. Ralph chose a roll, inserted it, sat on the highly polished stool and started to pedal. You should have seen the looks of amazement on the faces of not only the Aboriginal but also the white staff. Peals of laughter followed when Ralph and those close enough to read the words on the roll started singing 'Oh Danny Boy'.

48

Educating the children

Madeline had been my boys' governess at Gordon Downs, and Joanne followed at Wave Hill. In between I taught Anthony and David myself, but I always expected too much of them. Whenever visitors came knocking at our door, I'd bring them in for a cup of coffee and tell the boys to continue with their sums while I entertained. I should have hung a 'Do Not Disturb' sign, but Ralph thought this would be a little rude. By the time I'd return to the schoolroom, my pupils would be gone—off to play with Bronwyn and Sally Clark, and always very hard to find.

The Sydney Correspondence School was excellent, not only for Anthony but David too. They had a fantastic art course in their curriculum; for every painting that was set for the boys, they had to use live models. Sometimes one of the Aboriginal women would pose, sometimes me. Every week they did a painting and I still have them all filed away. Subjects included: *Woman Fumbling in Her Purse*—Old Ida, the Aboriginal lady from the soup kitchen, sitting on the floor and fumbling in her purse; *Woman Washing Her Hair*—me, and I looked ghastly.

Anthony was now eight years old and the last governess, Laura, had found teaching him to be very difficult. She gave up because he was just not interested. I had to take over and found it difficult too. After much thought, we decided to send him off to school. Believe me, it was an extremely hard decision to make.

We booked him into Our Lady of the Sacred Heart College (OLSH) in Bowral, in the highlands south of Sydney, which was run by nuns. Mum was not far away in Wollongong, where he would spend any free weekends. We'd receive very sad letters from Anthony, but he worked hard and the nuns were pleased with him.

A year later, David told us that he wanted to join Anthony at OLSH. We didn't want to send David, but he was so insistent that we gave in. Then, unfortunately, he was very miserable there. The boys claimed that they were given dog food to eat—you know how little boys carry on.

Jason went two years later. Ralph and I missed them terribly, but we wanted the best education for our children and at the time it was the way to go. The boys have never let me forget that they were only eight years old when they were sent to school down south. But I look back and see how independent they became.

However, when I think of Anthony having to go back to school by himself after his first holidays, I cringe. He left on a MacRobertson Miller Airline plane from Wave Hill to Alice

Springs, where a family friend picked him up and off-loaded him onto the Qantas plane to Adelaide. Then it was up to the hostesses and Anthony to get on the next two flights, to Melbourne and then to Sydney. My mother met him at Sydney Airport and drove him to his school in Bowral. What a different world it is today; children would rarely be allowed to travel by themselves. In those times it was relatively safe.

In 1970, before Jason went away to school, I booked him into the Katherine School of the Air, a distance education school under the control of the Northern Territory Department of Education. Until heading down south, the older boys had continued with Sydney Correspondence School, which we thought excellent. We believed at the time that there was no point in changing them to the Kimberley school when it became available.

A radio transmitter was supplied to Jason and lessons were sent out on the mail plane. Every day his teacher would communicate with her pupils, scattered around the northernmost part of the Territory. We would sing songs, have discussions, and read out stories the pupils had written. One song we loved was 'The Dying Stockman', with lyrics first published in 1885 and written by Horace Flower, a Queensland station owner. About this time there was a mobile 'caravan' school for both white and Aboriginal children with a teacher, Rosalie, who'd come to visit. But by then our children were away at school.

One day we heard that there was going to be a School of the Air gymkhana at Delamere Station, 350 kilometres away on the road to Katherine. I radioed Liz MacLeod of Delamere to ask, 'What can I bring?'

'A piglet for the greasy pig race,' Liz said.

No worries, there was a litter of piglets in our pigpen.

We must have looked a sight rolling up at Delamere with a caged piglet on the roof of our Land Rover station wagon. We greased the animal with fat before we let it go—then the children had to try and catch it. What a hullabaloo!

Jason rode a Delamere Station pony in the barrel and bending races. He even had his photo taken for *Hoofs & Horns* magazine.

The boys flew home every school holidays and loved going out to help pull bores with the bore mechanic, or to the stock camps with Ralph. They all had their slug guns and the crows became very wary. Standing targets, like fence posts and trees, became fair game too.

49

The problems of stress

From the time we'd arrived back at Wave Hill, Ralph had been trying to ignore a nagging pain in his abdomen. He didn't talk about it, but I knew there was something wrong. 'Oh no, nothing wrong with me,' he'd say. I would examine him and tell him he'd have to see the doctor on the next visit. And so it went on, the pain slowly worsening as the months passed by. Occasionally he'd vomit his food. Men can be so stubborn about their health issues! He was too busy worrying about the station, and not taking the time to worry about himself. And he was smoking heavily.

In the early hours one morning, Ralph had gone to the bathroom. I heard a crash. Jumping out of bed, I raced to investigate and found him lying on the floor leaning against the toilet bowl. 'Ralph, can you hear me?'

The reply was nothing more than a mumble. His pulse was very rapid. I tried to make him as comfortable as possible in the loo, then went to get help.

Tony and Matt managed to get Ralph into bed and he started to come around, but something serious had definitely occurred in his body. When daylight arrived I contacted Darwin Aerial Medical. Ralph was taken to Darwin Hospital, where he was diagnosed with a deep-seated duodenal ulcer. He was hospitalised for two weeks and advised to see a gastroenterologist when we went south, as the ulcer was likely to erode further and cause a rupture in his small bowel. He came home with antacids, and I'm sure he was on phenobarbital to relieve cyclic vomiting. It wasn't like today, when ulcers can be treated so quickly with acid-suppressing medication and one week of two different antibiotics.

On holidays two months later at the end of 1972, Ralph and I had an appointment to see a Macquarie Street specialist in Sydney. He recommended a major operation: half of Ralph's stomach would be removed and the other half joined to the duodenum, the first section of the small intestine. Ralph was admitted to Sydney Hospital where this operation was performed and thankfully went well.

During Ralph's time in hospital, I stayed with my brother Tony and his wife Moira in their unit at Randwick. Tony was no longer a priest. He'd finished his nine years of study to become a Passionist priest, then taken the name Father Fabian. He was sent to a hospital in Hobart to work with another priest as a hospital padre. He then decided, after all those years of study, that the priesthood wasn't for him, and left. This amazed everyone, but he obviously had his reasons. When I asked what they were, he just said, 'You wouldn't understand.' He went back to being an accountant and married Moira, a lovely widow with one child.

After ten days in hospital, Ralph was discharged and I took him to the unit. That night he complained of severe chest pains. They were so severe, he said, that he felt like jumping from the balcony. We were on the third floor. I was so worried; there was no emergency number like triple zero in those days, and I was a little apprehensive about ringing the surgeon when Ralph had only left the hospital ten hours before. But the surgeon said, 'Bring him straight in.'

So, at two in the morning, Tony drove us back to Sydney Hospital. I thought Ralph was having a coronary—so did the surgeon. The pain must have been excruciating as it turned out to be pericarditis, inflammation of the muscles around the heart that stretch with every heartbeat. This was caused by a virus from an infected bag of blood that he'd been given after his surgery.

For several days he was on the critical list. Upset, anxious and thinking the worst, I decided to go and pick up the children so he could see them. Jason, six years old, was staying in Wollongong with my mother; Anthony and David, ten and eight, were at OLSH. I collected them in the new Ford Fairlane that Ralph and I had purchased earlier in the holidays, and brought them back to see their dad. That was the turning point: after seeing them, Ralph started to improve.

My husband needed more time to recuperate. Mum offered to look after him for another month, while Anthony and David went back to school and Jason and I went back on our own. Knowing Ralph, he would have driven all the way to Wave and then started work as soon as he returned, so I accepted Mum's offer on his behalf. Jason and I were to drive back with Pat and Gus Ringler, who'd been on holidays in Sydney at the same time as us. We arranged to meet at Bowral. Mum and Ralph were coming to see us off.

The morning of departure we were up at 5 a.m. It was still dark outside. I was in the bathroom shaving my legs, with one leg in the washbasin. Suddenly there was the sound of an explosion from deep down in the earth. The lights went out. The building shook and trembled. I knew at once that it was an earth tremor or quake. In Wollongong, of all places!

'Quick, Ralph, get Mum and I'll grab Jason!' I yelled out, as we stumbled to the door. We rushed to a vacant allotment on one side of the units.

As the sun came up, the residents from the other units in the building, woken by the tremor, emerged from doorways facing the allotment. There we were, all huddled together. I suddenly remembered, as I noticed everyone staring at me, that I only had a bra and underpants on. 'Hurry, Jason, stand in front of me,' I said, feeling highly embarrassed as I pulled him over to shield me.

Half an hour later, normality restored, we were on the road to Bowral to meet Pat and Gus and continue our journey to the Territory. I know Ralph hated having to stay in Wollongong—but he needed time to recuperate before taking on his management role again.

In separate cars, Pat and Gus and Jason and I drove through Goulburn, Griffith, Hay, Mildura and Broken Hill. On reaching Port Augusta we, together with our cars, boarded the train to Alice Springs. What a relief to relax on the train for four days, and what a difference to my last trip through South Australia in 1960 in the minibuses with the CSIRO crew.

We arrived in Alice early in the morning. After breakfast we decided to walk into town, as our cars wouldn't be unloaded for some hours. We were wandering through the CBD when we came to the Alice Springs Hotel. Who should exit the front door but Roy Bell, the Vestey general manager, and Ces Watts, the pastoral inspector.

After greetings, Roy said to Jason, who was six at the time, 'How was your holiday?'

'Very good, thank you, Mr Bell. We had an earthquake in Wollongong and Mummy ran outside without her clothes on.'

For months afterwards, whenever Roy was at Wave and we had new visitors, he'd say, 'Did you hear about the earthquake in Wollongong and Thea running outside without her clothes on?'

I had to laugh and so did everyone else.

An old friend, Tony Guerner, who'd been a jackaroo with Ralph at Wave before my time, offered to fly him back after he'd recuperated. Tony and Ralph were great friends, and we'd often visited him and his wife, Vickie, at their property Yarrawin in Brewarrina.

So Tony flew Ralph back to us. He looked so much better and it was so good to have him home.

After staying at Wave for a few days, Tony said, 'Who do you want to visit in the Territory? I'll take you there.'

Jason was the only child at home, so he came with us. We flew to Gordon Downs to see Madeline, Milton, and their now three children, and on to Katherine to visit Lynn and Patsy. Lynn had started a butcher shop in town, and was also supplying the nearby Tindall Air Force Base with gravel. He was making a fortune! We then flew in to Nutwood Downs Station, where Sue and Tony Clark and their daughters were now based.

Throughout our journey, Jason wasn't well. He developed a temperature. When we returned home, his breathing became rapid and stertorous, deep and laboured. We grew very worried. In the early hours, after getting onto a doctor in Katherine, Tony Guerner flew me and Jason into town at the very low altitude of 150 metres in order to maintain Jason's oxygen levels.

Dr Jim Scattini was waiting for us at the hospital. After an X-ray revealed double pneumonia, Jason was commenced on intravenous antibiotics. We were so lucky. Thanks to Tony Guerner and Dr Scattini, he made a wonderful recovery.

50

A penny for our thoughts

In 1973 we procured a grey pony for David's tenth birthday. She was a frisky little thing called Moonlight. David, a competent horse rider, came off Moonlight and fractured his left femur, and the Aerial Medical Service transported him to Darwin. As only the patient was allowed on the flight, I had to find a lift. Luckily, someone in a truck came through Wave Hill at the time, heading in the right direction. I was pregnant, expecting my fourth child, but it didn't worry me going to Darwin by truck—I was just anxious to get there for David. This pregnancy was a lovely surprise, as it had been eight years since Jason was born.

David was in Darwin Hospital for two weeks. I stayed with friends, getting lifts to the hospital every day. He was then transferred to Katherine.

I remember giving him his school lessons, which the nuns from OLSH had sent up. David was in no mood to do schoolwork; I tried cajoling him, but it didn't have much effect.

So we played games, read stories, and David wrote letters to his grandmothers. There he was, a very active ten-year-old, confined to bed for six weeks.

Not long after David and I returned from hospital, him on crutches and me heavily pregnant, we had to start preparing to head for Sydney, where I was to have my baby. Jason was coming with me and David, because this was when we'd decided to send him to school with the other boys—what horrible parents!

Ralph drove me and the boys to Darwin. What a pathetic bunch we looked, a pregnant woman escorting two little boys, one on crutches.

For some reason the plane had to go via Cairns where there was a curfew, and we had to stay the night. Being a pessimist, before I left Darwin I made sure that my doctor notified a good obstetrician in Cairns, just in case I went into labour. Well, you never know! Nothing happened, of course.

Mum picked Anthony up at OLSH and met us at Bondi Beach, where I had a unit booked for the school holidays. We had an exciting time beside the sea at Bondi, visiting Luna Park and Taronga Zoo, and going to movies, although the boys were just as happy watching TV in the unit, a great novelty for them. At Wave, as well as all over the Territory, there was no TV except for in Darwin and Alice Springs, and this was 1974. We depended on the radio for world news. Ralph and I didn't even know what or who The Beatles were until one of our Sydney visits coincided with their first trip to Australia.

At the end of the holidays, Anthony and David went back to school, and Jason went for his first term. A week later I was admitted into Crown Street Hospital to spend the night before my third caesarean. Once again, the wonderful Dr John MacBeth was my obstetrician.

I was sure I was going to have another boy, but I was still hoping for a girl. A fellow in the Bondi chemist shop had looked at my protruding belly and announced for all to hear, 'Lady, you are going to have a boy.' That night at the hospital I wandered around to the nursery, counting the number of newborns: eighteen. I noticed that the boys far outnumbered the girls, twelve to six. *Wow!* I thought. *Maybe I have a chance of having a girl after all.*

On 12 September, my baby was born. Unlike today, one had a full anaesthetic during a caesar. I regained consciousness in my room, and low and behold there was Ralph. He'd flown down that morning from Darwin to surprise me; it was the first delivery he had attended. And he was trying to tell me something.

'It's a girl!' he kept saying.

In my fuddled state I thought I must be dreaming. Then I couldn't believe it. But it was true—Penny had finally arrived! How wonderful. We'd talked of the name Penny for twelve years. Maybe it was now a little old hat, we thought. Mum had said how she loved the name Sarah, so we'd decided to call the baby Sarah Penelope. But as soon as I saw her, it had to be Penny.

What a hit Penny was with all the stockmen and others on

our return to the station three weeks later. She was a beautiful baby. Life was perfect.

Anna and Cowboy Collins, Lynn's in-laws and our good friends from Katherine, came out to Wave Hill for Penny's christening, Anna to be godmother. We hadn't decided on the godfather, and upon mentioning this fact to the staff, we were inundated with volunteers. Penny ended up having one godmother and nine godfathers—anything to keep the peace!

Father Nicholas, the priest from Wyndham, came to officiate the christening, although we were hoping to have Father Michael Banks from Katherine, who'd recently put on a beautiful christening service at Kirkimbie Station.

Father Banks was very much like Father Flynn, who'd married me and Ralph: caring and compassionate but lots of fun. He was also young and extremely handsome, which was quite detrimental to his vocation. We heard that all the young women in Katherine were chasing the poor father, and unfortunately for us he found it a bit too much. Leaving both Katherine and the priesthood, he moved to Adelaide, married and divorced.

Many years later, my sister-in-law Patsy Hayes, who was then sadly a widow, was shopping in Darwin when she heard a familiar voice in a neighbouring shop. It was Michael Banks! Cupid shot his arrow and now they're happily married and living in Queensland.

51

Christmas 1974

When we first moved out to the new Wave Hill, we were asked by the Bureau of Meteorology to start a weather station. This was to be a completely self-contained, solar-powered unit, with wet and dry thermometers, a hygrometer for measuring relative humidity, a wind-speed propeller, a wind sock for direction, and a book of instructions plus pictures of the different cloud types. We were told the weather station was to be built on a site clear of trees and shrubs; the perfect site was across from the office, next to the last cottage.

I volunteered to be the weather lady. Reading times were 6 a.m., 9 a.m., 3 p.m. and 3 a.m., and I sent the results on the two-way radio. I did the 3 a.m. readings for a couple of weeks and would take Dasher to the weather station with me. However, this encouraged every dog in Wave to come out barking, so I gave those readings away.

*

Darling Dasher had reached the ripe old age of fourteen years. He'd been suffering from arthritis and would get cranky when he was brushed, objecting to having the knots pulled out of his long white hair. The heat had never worried him but now he was becoming stressed frequently.

The Katherine vet, on one of his regular visits, said, 'When Dasher starts moaning at night, the time will have come to have him put down.'

That's what happened on the vet's next visit. I cried for days. I felt the same as if I'd put down a family member. Dasher was a gorgeous dog.

We bought a new puppy, Pluto, a bullmastiff cross Rhodesian ridgeback.

At six in the morning on Christmas Day 1974, the weather was already hot and dry. With Pluto in tow, bouncing his large puppy body around me, I walked briskly to the weather station.

Looking up at the sky, I noted the types of clouds—both 'cirrus', thin clouds scattered high across the sky, and 'cumulus', puffy clouds below six thousand feet. More clouds than usual. *More rain coming*, I thought. I opened the weather box to read the barometer and the wet and dry thermometers, then checked the wind sock before veering across the flat to the office and its radio transmitter.

Letting myself in, I sat down at the desk, worked out the code for the weather report and turned on the transmitter. A lot of crackling followed. I picked up the microphone. 'Eight Oscar Golf, Eight Oscar Golf, calling Darwin Meteorology.

Eight Oscar Golf, calling Darwin Meteorology.' *Crackle, Crackle*. 'Where are you, Darwin? Eight Golf Oscar, 8OG, 8OG. Can you read? Can you read?'

Probably too much partying last night, I thought. *And to think I got up so early on Christmas morning!*

At about 11 a.m. we heard the news: the devastating Cyclone Tracy had hit Darwin. Tracy was a severe tropical cyclone with gale-force winds that killed seventy-one people and flattened seventy per cent of the town's buildings, leaving many homeless.

Imagine how I felt, having thought so badly of them. I remembered the weather I'd noticed that morning. Extra clouds, yes, but no inkling of a cyclone in the north—well, we were 800-odd kilometres away.

Ralph and Gus went up to Darwin a few days later. Gus to check on damage to Vestey properties: their office downtown and the pastoral inspector's house. Ralph to check on our investment three-bedroom house at Fannie Bay, which we'd bought a few years previously. It was a very good buy in a great suburb, with a timber and steel frame on stilts.

The pastoral inspector and his wife, Ces and Dawn Watts, had sheltered in their bathroom on that terrible Christmas Eve, as their home at Bullocky Point had disintegrated around them.

Ralph was pleased to find our Fannie Bay house intact except for a missing roof. He and Gus dropped their gear at the house and went off to register, as was required, with the

Cyclone Committee. When they returned, all their gear and our whitegoods had gone. Stolen! There was a lot of thievery after the cyclone.

We were very lucky with that house. After having the insurance company put on a new roof, we then sold it at an excellent price the following year.

We weren't strangers to extreme weather on Wave Hill, though had experienced nothing like Darwin's cyclone. Some time after Cyclone Tracy, Ralph and the staff decided to hold a rodeo at Wave. It was to be on Boxing Day and Ralph invited all the neighbouring stations to join in.

Jimmy Stretton was the cook and, as quite a few people had decided to come, he'd been left back at the homestead to prepare lunch. The bamboo blinds rattled, and rattled, and Jimmy wondered what was happening. He realised that the slight breeze had become a very strong wind that was getting stronger and stronger. He was thinking, *It can't be a storm on a beautiful day like this.*

Down at the yards the rest of the station folk, white and Aboriginal, were having a wonderful time, eskies in tow: some sitting on the roof of the shed; some on deckchairs on the back of the truck with brollies for shade; others perched on the rails. All were watching, with excitement, the bareback bronco riders performing.

Suddenly, out of the clear sky appeared a huge dark cloud. At the same time, a ferocious wind with the force of a hurricane whipped across the yard, pushing the spectators off the roof and the people on chairs off the back of the truck. Everyone cowered in the shelter of the yard posts or under the vehicles.

The tornado only lasted a few minutes, but was devastating in its narrow path. The school caravan was on its side with all the equipment wrecked. In the domestic quarters, an inner wall had collapsed. There were branches scattered everywhere with many trees uprooted.

Thoughts of how Darwin had suffered during Cyclone Tracy made everyone think how lucky we were.

52

The Handover

16 August 1975

PROGRAM

The Administrator of the Northern Territory,
His Honour, Mr J.N. Nelson.

The Minister for Aboriginal Affairs,
the Honourable Les Johnson, M.P.

Mr Roger Golding, General Manager, Angliss Group

The Prime Minister of Australia,
the Honourable Gough Whitlam, Q.C., M.P.

Mr Vincent Lingiari representing Gurindji people

Messages of Goodwill

Luncheon including entertainment arranged by
Gurindji people

'Thea, go and save Margaret,' uttered Roy Bell, the Vestey general manager.

Behind us, at the rear of the elevated seating, we saw Margaret Whitlam, the prime minister's wife, surrounded by Aboriginal women and children, all trying to catch her attention. They wanted to talk to this 'Missus' whose husband was about to return part of their land to them. Margaret seemed a little embarrassed at all the attention as she kept glancing at the program in her hand and then moved off to be with her husband.

There was a sense of occasion, a deep feeling of a major event happening in Australia. We, the Vestey crowd—Roy Bell, Ces Watts, Mr Roger Golding as Lord Vestey's representative, Ralph, me, Anthony and Penny—were sitting on the elevated seats awaiting the ceremony.

There were about 350 people there, more Aboriginals than whites.

This day was the culmination of years of what we at the cattle station called the 'Experiment Wave Hill'. Daguragu had become like an anthropology campus at a university. In fact, uni students had come out and helped the Aboriginal residents build mudbrick houses and plant orange trees. Meanwhile, every aspect of the Gurindji people's lives had been picked apart as if they were scientific exhibits.

When we'd first arrived for the handover and strolled across from our vehicle, we met the nurse who had lived with the Gurindji people for part of their nine-year struggle. Ralph had only met her once before. She said to him, 'Stop scowling,

Ralph,' but unbeknownst to her he often looked like that when he was serious.

He ignored her and turned to a *Sydney Morning Herald* journalist who was hovering about, waiting for an interview. Ralph said to her, 'Look around you and see what has been achieved in nine years for a few million dollars.'

His brief interaction with the nurse and his comment to the journalist were duly published in the *Sydney Morning Herald* article about the handover.

Putting everything into context, it's easy to recant—but this was the 1970s and at the time I supported what my husband said. I do think he could have been a little more circumspect with so many members of the metropolitan press around.

After the walk-off, a lot of time and money had poured into Daguragu from all over Australia to help the Gurindji people. But it was not in the make-up of the Gurindji to be sedentary, to build houses and grow crops. They were a largely nomadic people. Ralph had a lot of time for the Aboriginal people, but he was worried that without continued guidance and support, the money would all be wasted.

On the day of the handover, the country at Daguragu looked very tired. There were only a few spindly trees, and the main buildings were humpies in the background. The Australian flag flew beside a tarpaulin that was connected to an old corrugated lean-to. On top of the lean-to was a sign that read: 'Gurindji Mining Lease and Cattle Station'.

Aboriginal children and dogs were running through the lean-to, while Vincent Lingiari, Dexter Daniels and other tribal elders stood waiting for the important moment. Vincent looked old and weary, but he stood tall in his new shirt and jeans. Tables were set with paper plates and plastic cutlery for the barbecue to follow the ceremony. The Gurindji women were ready for their corroboree, and in deference to the occasion had put on bras instead of being topless.

Not far from the lean-to, Prime Minister Gough Whitlam, the Minister for Aboriginal Affairs and other dignitaries all looked hot and uncomfortable in their business suits as they stood around waiting. Suddenly Margaret moved over to her husband and they entered the shade of the tarpaulin with the other VIPs.

The Vestey representative Roger Golding stood in front of the microphone with Vincent to his right. He was the first to speak, promising four hundred head of cattle to mark the occasion and as a token of the company's goodwill towards its neighbour. Vincent looked very pleased and I could see smiles from some of the Aboriginal people standing nearby.

Then the prime minister came forward. He made a short speech about giving back ownership of the land, '1250 square miles'. Wave Hill had been leased land: the region given to the Gurindji was taken off the Vestey lease. The government paid for new fencing; and, as it was difficult to fence in and out of the river, they provided a block without river frontage and put down four or five bores.

The deeds were then handed over as proof that this land now belonged to the Gurindji people. Gough Whitlam bent down, picked up a handful of sand and poured it into Vincent's hand, saying that it was a sign of the restoration of the land to his people. Vincent looked quite overcome and hung his head, gazing down at the sand. Even the kids were quiet.

Then Vincent, in his humble way, started chanting in Gurindji, talking to his people. Finally he said, 'We are all right now. We all friendly. We are mates.'

There was silence. Everyone was overcome by this most moving speech.

Vincent Lingiari's fight for his people's rights made him a national figure, and in 1976 he was named a Member of the Order of Australia for his services to the Aboriginal people. His story is celebrated in the song 'From Little Things Big Things Grow', written by Paul Kelly and the Indigenous musician Kev Carmody.

When I'd first come to Wave, on the wall in Tom Fisher's office hung a brass Aboriginal breastplate, its inscription reading 'JIMMY/KING of WAVE HILL'. It was crescent-shaped, flat in a vertical plane, with a chain attached at each apex.

Breastplates were presented to Aboriginal people by Europeans from the earliest times of colonisation. Governments and pastoralists gave breastplates to the men and women they considered the leaders in an area. In this way they hoped to use Aboriginal leaders to control their own people.

Before Tom retired, he presented Ralph with the Wave Hill breastplate. The name inscribed, 'Jimmy', refers to Vincent Lingiari's grandfather, an elder of the Gurindji tribe in the early twentieth century. The breastplate was offered to Vincent before it was given to Ralph, but he declined it because of its association with the Vestey Group.

This Aboriginal breastplate is now at the Museum and Art Gallery of the Northern Territory in Darwin.

Picnic at Moonbull
Waterhole at Kirkimbie
Station, NT.
Thea, Ralph, Robyn,
Anthony, Cameron
and Graham Fulcher,
Anthony and David,
1965.

Penny dancing in the
orchard at Wave Hill.

Baby Jason on the lawn at Gordon
Downs with Thea and Skippy, 1965.

The bookmakers at the Negri Race Meeting waiting to take bets from the lovely ladies of the Outback.

Everyone loaded up and heading off to the Negri Races.

Our bush camp at Negri Race Meeting was set up with a kitchen and sleeping areas.

Baker Dollie's children in the vegetable garden at Wave Hill, 1961.

Swimming pool, Outback style! Anthony and David at Gordon Downs Station, 1966.

Thea and Anthony at Gordon Downs.

Thea and baby David, 1963.

Bridesmaid Thea and best man Ralph at Heather and Rod Russell's wedding at Limbunya Station, 1961.

A very moving moment. Prime Minister Gough Whitlam pours soil into the hand of Vincent Lingiari in a gesture to symbolise the handing back of Gurindji land. (Photo courtesy of Ces Watts).

'Anthony, stand over there next to Gough Whitlam and I'll take your photo!' From left to right: Gordon Bryant, Bill Wentworth (at rear), Nugget Coombes, Gough Whitlam, Anthony, unknown journalist.

Prime Minister Gough Whitlam with the Vestey's representative from England, Roger Golding, at the Handover ceremony.

The new Wave Hill station from the air, 1968.

"EQUAL WAGES FOR ABORIGINES"
"THERE MUST BE AN END TO WAGE DISCRIMINATION"

- This was a resolution concerning Aborigines passed at the 1963 A.C.T.U. Congress.

- The award rate for adult male Aborigines working in the pastoral industry in the N.T. is £2/8/3 per week plus keep (or £2/13/- in lieu of keep). The corresponding amounts for adult females are £1/5/3 and 16/6 in lieu of keep. Note that the TOTAL weekly wage of these Aborigines is less than the INCREASE being sought by the A.C.T.U.

Extract from a newspaper article reporting on the Gurindji walkout from Wave Hill Station.

The photos on this page show some of the staff on Wave Hill Station in 1979. At left are Mosquito and Connie.

Vera (who worked in the laundry), her husband, Oscar, and their children.

Dora and Charlie outside the men's quarters.

Thea, aged 19, on a jetty at the Dame Edith Walker Nursing Home where nurses from Royal Prince Alfred Hospital were sent to work for a few months.

Thea at her 70th birthday, celebrated in Brisbane.

There were hugs and smiles all around when Thea recently returned to visit. To the right of Thea are Mary-Anne, Biddy and Pansy, and Topsy on the left.

53

Well-intentioned men

The manager of Victoria River Downs Station in the 1960s told me that there were ninety thousand head of cattle on the property before World War II, then all the men went off to fight and the cattle had been out of hand ever since. 'Micky' bulls (young, uncastrated bulls) were everywhere. Helicopter mustering started in 1968 because a Mr Pat Shaw agreed to have a go. Yards were built, a helicopter purchased, and, slowly, aerial mustering grew.

During the 1970s beef crash, stations were looking for cost-saving methods of mustering. Numbers of ex-Vietnam pilots were looking for flying jobs. Then the Brucellosis & Tuberculosis Eradication Campaign cranked up and all cattle had to be mustered.

When helicopter mustering started at Wave Hill, not long after the handover, a company called Heli-Muster, run by John Weymouth, came to stay with its helicopters, pilots and engineers. Later John went to Delamere Station and was replaced by Tony Ferris, who came with his wife, Lisa, and their daughter, Erinca. Penny and Erinca became the best of friends and had lots of fun playing together.

Ralph used to go out mustering with Tony every day, giving advice, and he was always ready with a gun in case of a rogue beast. One evening Lisa and I were still waiting for their return after the evening meal, which was unusual. We started to get worried that something serious had happened, when in they walked. Thank goodness! A small hiccough with the chopper.

One day when our boys were due home for the Christmas holidays and I was preparing to drive in to Katherine and pick them up, Tony said, 'Thea, I can fly you to Katherine, pick up the boys and bring them home.'

I thought that sounded wonderful.

The Sydney plane didn't get in till 5 p.m., and it was running late. The boys had a large suitcase each; as it was the end of the year, they'd brought their entire wardrobe home. Undaunted, Tony placed the suitcases on the back seat of the four-seater Heli-Muster Cessna. The boys sat on top and away we went. The plane was so overloaded we had trouble getting off the ground—but we made it.

The next worry was the light, which was definitely fading. The sun was going down and, for me, panic was setting in. How were we to land in the dark? Tony could see my concern. As we flew closer to Delamere, Tony said, 'Would you like to spend the night here and continue to Wave in the morning?'

I could have hugged him on the spot—a bit difficult when he was flying! Down we went, landing at Delamere to find that John Weymouth was entertaining our ex-general manager, Mr Peter Morris. We had a very enjoyable evening with great company, and a safe journey to Wave Hill in the morning.

One of our young stockmen, Brian 'Bigfoot' Gettens, was keen to obtain his fixed-wing flying licence, which he did on his holidays. He returned to Wave Hill in someone's plane; I've forgotten whose. He offered me and Ralph a trip out to neighbouring Cattle Creek. I felt quite nervous at the thought of flying with such a new recruit, but didn't have the heart to say no.

We took Penny with us, leaving the boys at home. I thought if worst came to worst, I wasn't going to leave my baby motherless.

As we came in to land the plane at Cattle Creek, it hit a wet patch on the airstrip and we started to slide. Bigfoot had told us to open the doors as we landed; I don't know why. Water and mud shot through. I thought that this was it—we were going to crash! I screamed in terror. But Bigfoot controlled the plane beautifully. We slowed up and came safely to a stop. I realised he was a very good, safe pilot. The flight back was without mishap.

Bigfoot went on to get his helicopter licence. He mustered on the big cattle stations throughout the Territory, then flew for Kerry Packer and Channel Nine in Sydney for many years.

We had another scary moment, a couple of years later.

One of the stockmen asked Ralph if he could leave his rifle in our house while he went on holidays. Ralph said, 'Yes, put it in the linen room,' which was just off the entrance foyer.

Our boys came home for the holidays. They were on one side of the house, in their bedrooms. We were in the lounge room on the other side, relaxing and entertaining friends, when we heard a rifle shot. Racing around to the boys' rooms, we discovered Anthony standing there in shock.

He'd found the rifle and taken it to show David and Jason. 'Stick 'em up!' he said, as he pointed it at David and pulled the trigger. The bullet went through the wall, inches from David's head.

A lesson to us all.

54

The horse sale

In 1975 the Vesteys held a horse sale at Wave Hill. They were selling their horse brand for the first time, as there were too many horses on the station. The pastoral inspector, Ces Watts, contacted Jock Bremner, an agent in Darwin. Ces flew the agent down to Wave two weeks before the sale to go through the horses with Ralph and draw up a catalogue.

Six hundred horses were for sale: stock horses, breakers, brood mares and foals. The Vesteys had always kept immaculate horse books and only bought the best sires in the country. The sale attracted buyers from all over Australia. Jock spent four days on the radiotelephone sending the horse details to his secretary in Darwin, as twelve minutes was the maximum allowed in one phone call.

Sale day came and about three hundred people arrived, bringing swags, grog and food. A bullock was killed for the occasion. Our friend Ben Humphreys arrived with his hawker van to do the catering. Ben had been coming to the Territory for many years and later sold out of his hawker business. After he retired from hawking, he joined the Labor party and became Minister for Veterans' Affairs from 1987 to 1993. At our horse sale Ben brought with him Jimmy Stretton, an old friend of his from Brisbane who was an excellent cook.

Two other friends of ours, Patricia and Grey Lapthorne, had flown in from the Gold Coast. Someone organised a 'blue movie'. When the lights went out in the marquee where the movie was showing, Patricia and I crept into the back area to satisfy our curiosity. We got more than we bargained for and fled in horror.

The sale went on for three days, starting at eight-thirty each morning and finishing at three each afternoon. Every horse was sold, and they went to every state in Australia except Tasmania. At the conclusion of the sale there was only an hour and a half to draft six hundred horses. Ralph offered Jock the assistance of the jackaroos, but he preferred the Aboriginal stockmen— especially Algie, Emilie's husband, who knew every foal and which mare it belonged to.

By the fourth day, with the exception of Jimmy Stretton, they were all gone, even Ben Humphreys. As we were desperate for a station cook, Jimmy decided to stay and take the position.

55

The cat

The chookyard was in our backyard. I had hens, ducks, a drake and many ducklings. As I was walking down there one morning, David put his head out the window and said, 'Mum, Daphne's cat Tinker is trying to kill your ducklings.'

Daphne was the bookkeeper. A single lady, she'd come to Australia from South Africa and had been with us for several years.

'David, it's okay,' I said, 'the cat can't get in to the ducklings. The chook pen is very secure.' I trotted off to do the nursing.

The next day, Daphne came into the clinic. 'Thea, would you mind having a look at Tinker? She isn't well and she isn't eating.'

I had a sudden horrible feeling, recalling yesterday's talk with David.

'No, of course not!' I said. 'Bring her down here.'

While I examined the cat, Daphne told me how well Tinker had been until that morning, when she'd had slightly loose bowels.

'Daphne,' I said, 'I shall ring the vet in Katherine, give him the signs and symptoms, and see what he says.'

I felt quite relieved when the vet said that Tinker probably had feline enteritis, and he would send out some tablets on the mail plane.

That evening, Ralph and I and the boys were sitting in our kitchen, chatting, when Daphne arrived. 'I've discovered a little hole in Tinker's side,' she said.

'How very odd,' I said.

'What do you think it is?'

'I've no idea, but I'll come down and have a look at her.'

Ralph was being very quiet.

Down I went to Daphne's quarters. Lying on a mat in her kitchen was Tinker. I knelt beside the cat and started feeling her abdomen with my hand. I found the hole. It was about two to three millimetres across. 'Yes, I've found it,' I said. 'It's very strange.'

'What?!' Daphne said, looking from the cat to me. 'Is there one on that side too?'

Shock horror! Someone had shot Daphne's cat. At that moment I knew we were guilty. There was nothing I could say except how sorry and sad I was, knowing that one of my children was responsible. Ralph had, meanwhile, guessed correctly what was wrong with the cat.

At midnight there was a rapid tapping on our bedroom window. It was Daphne again. We weren't going to get off lightly.

'Tinker is dying,' she sobbed. 'You must come down to see her.'

The cat

Poor Daphne! Down we went. It was just after midnight and we stayed until the very end, and the poor animal breathed its last.

I was very angry as I gathered the children together the next morning, and asked, 'Who shot Daphne's cat?'

David hung his head. Anthony and Jason had smirks on their faces and said nothing.

'Okay,' I said, 'I'm going to get Ralph.'

'David, own up!' said Anthony.

'You're the one who killed her,' said Jason.

'David, are you responsible for killing Daphne's cat?' I asked.

'Well, she was trying to kill your ducklings, Mum.'

'What a terrible thing to do, David. Daphne loved that cat. Now you're coming up to the office to tell her that you're really sorry.'

Up we went to the bookkeeper's office.

'Daphne, David has something to say to you,' I said.

David stood, head hanging down. 'I'm sorry I killed your cat,' he mumbled with a grin on his face, which I was hoping she wouldn't see, but I'm sure she did.

Daphne hardly spoke to me for the next six months.

56

Success at last

Ralph was always very involved with our yearly race meeting at the Negri. The meetings were still meant to be grass-fed affairs, which Ralph duly stuck to, even though we heard that others were grain-feeding their horses. Consequently, we were lucky to get a third or fourth place in any race.

On holidays one year, we went to visit my cousin Gwen Cunningham and her husband, John, in Ben Lomond, New South Wales. Paddy, one of their sons, was also visiting; at that time, he was the leading apprentice jockey in the Grafton area.

'Hey, young fellow,' Ralph said to Paddy, 'how about coming up to Wave Hill and working for me?'

Being adventurous, Paddy thought this a great idea and arrived at Wave shortly afterwards. He went into one of the stock camps. Ralph made sure that our best racehorses were handy for Paddy to train.

That year we went over to the Negri Races on the Monday;

Tuesday was meet and greet day. On Tuesday night, we all went to the drawing of the Calcutta, in which everyone buys tickets in the hope of drawing a horse. Next the horses are auctioned off to the highest bidder. If you draw a horse, you can buy it at half the auction price, while if anyone else wants to buy it, they pay full price. The money raised is then divided between the first prize (sixty per cent), second (thirty per cent) and third (ten per cent)—which, depending on the auction, can each be worth lots of money.

The night of the Calcutta, the bar was open and the stockmen were gearing up to let their hair down and have a few beers. This included Paddy. I thought that with the big race day tomorrow, he would be better off coming back to the camp with us. He readily agreed, then hopped in one door of our car and hopped out the other!

Ralph just said, 'Don't worry, he'll be fine.'

The next day—the first race day—everyone arrived dressed in their best clothes: ladies with their hats, gloves and high-heeled shoes; gentlemen looking very dapper. The bookies were in position, taking bets on the first race. Everyone moved to the grandstand as the horses came out of the holding yard and trotted to the gates. Then they were off!

Coming down the straight was Paddy on our horse, Diana Dors. He was coming up fast, past Sabrina, and nearly at the winning post. There he was, Paddy on Diana Dors, coming in first! I was jumping up and down in delight, surrounded by ladies congratulating me with hugs and kisses.

In the second race he did it again! This time there was only a smidgen of a congratulatory murmur from those around me, a single peck on the cheek.

After the third race and following wins, no one wanted to know me. We won all the races. It was fantastic!

Ralph was president of the Negri that year, which meant I'd been in charge of buying all the trophy prizes, so some weeks earlier I'd purchased them in Darwin. Naturally I bought things that I really liked: silver—EPNS, really—ice buckets and silver wine glasses, to name a couple.

Presentation night was exciting and rather embarrassing, with Ralph presenting me with all the trophies. But we loved it, after all those years of winning next to nothing.

57

The social club

Not long after we moved to the new Wave Hill, the staff requested the right to have a drink in the evening and at the weekend. Times were a-changin'—dry stations were a thing of the past. After contacting head office, we were allowed to start a social club.

Every evening before dinner, those who wished could buy two drinks at the bar. It was a fun get-together at the end of the day. On Saturday night, six drinks were allowed. We returned to the rec room after dinner, played ping-pong, darts or billiards, or just socialised. Sometimes we played cards: mainly five hundred, which the older stockmen loved. All visitors to the station at the weekend were able to enjoy our social club.

Every fortnight a movie would arrive from Darwin on the mail plane. It would be shown on the back wall of the kitchen. Bringing chairs, blankets and maybe a packet of lollies from the store, everyone—Aboriginals and whites—would settle down to a great evening. If it was an exceptional film we would show it again, as we had a week between each plane. We watched *Cabaret* three times.

In 1971, Fred Hollows came to Wave with his ophthalmic team to test all the Aboriginal residents for trachoma, an infectious bacterial disease that causes a roughening of the eyelids, and the leading cause of infectious blindness in the world. Fred wasn't well known then. He was a very pleasant and dedicated ophthalmologist who worked with the Gurindji people at Daguragu, as well as at the station, and assisted in the establishment of medical services for Aboriginal people throughout Australia.

There were four in his team, two nurses and two doctors. We told them about Saturday night in the rec room, so they joined us for a drink after dinner. My brother-in-law Lynn and Swannie—who'd been working on Wave for years—must have had a few too many before they arrived, as they dared each other to strip off and do a streak around the rec room.

And that's exactly what they did! When I think about it now, I am mortified. I was annoyed with them at the time but couldn't stop laughing, especially at the look on some of our visitors' faces. I bet that the Fred Hollows team didn't forget Wave Hill in a hurry.

Sometime in the seventies, the Aboriginal residents were allowed to purchase beer from the social club on a Saturday night. The men and women would line up outside the rec room, waiting for their six cans each. In the beginning, the men made such a mess of themselves. As the women hardly drank, their husbands would often drink the full dozen. The results were arguments, fights, split heads, lacerations and occasionally broken limbs—a busy time for the nursing sister.

One Christmas morning, Ralph was busy dealing with Aboriginal arguments. I was called to the hospital: 'Mad' Maria's husband had hit her on top of her head with a nulla-nulla, inflicting a large wound that was squirting blood like a fountain. It was impossible for me to stitch, so I applied pressure until the plane arrived. I couldn't leave her for about an hour as it kept seeping blood.

Finally, when the flow eased, I made her husband sit and press on the dressing while I went back to check on my boys. To my dismay, the little devils had opened every parcel under the Christmas tree. Gifts and cards were all jumbled up, and I would never know who'd sent what. I felt like crying.

Whenever there were conflicts between the Aboriginal residents, they would come up to the homestead to tell 'dat Ralph' or 'Ralphie' their troubles. Ralph loved helping to sort out their problems.

One morning I came back to the homestead from the clinic to find one of the kitchen girls, Connie, drunk and raving on to Ralph. He was sitting on the front steps, thoroughly enjoying this banter, while Connie stood in the middle of the pathway. I'd just had a very busy morning attending to the results of fights in the settlement; I was in no mood for any more intoxicated Aboriginal people. I said, and I'd never used these words before, 'Piss off, Connie!'

She nearly collapsed in shock at me saying such a rude thing. 'You no talk like dat. You da missus!' But she did take off to the sound of Ralph's peals of laughter. I felt so ashamed.

Every year, Christmas dinner was held in the rec room and catered for thirty to forty people. The tables were set in long rows adorned with bonbons, red-and-green serviettes and decorations. At that time, Cold Duck was the favourite celebratory alcoholic drink for the ladies; it tasted a little like champagne. The men, of course, drank beer.

One Christmas morning, I woke to find that the cap on my front tooth had fallen out and was lying on my pillow. We were expecting important visitors that day, and there I was with a front tooth missing. Horror!

Prior to my marriage, I'd had a friendly argument with the stockman Jim Tough over a jar of macadamia nuts, a gift from some visitor. He was trying to wrench the jar out of my hand. As I pulled away, he suddenly let go and the lid slammed into my mouth, breaking my central right tooth. Devastation!

I had to go to Darwin to see the dentist, and he filled the slanted broken half with gold. I'd implored him to use anything *but*—however, this was Darwin, a frontier town. So that was it, I thought, I would never smile again!

I'd had the part-gold tooth for about ten years when the cap fell out.

Waking Ralph up, I said, 'Look! How can I appear in public like this?'

But my husband had the solution. Not that I was very happy about it, but I was desperate. He sealed my cap into place, and do you know what he used? Araldite glue. It's a wonder it didn't make me sick. That cap stayed put for at least another five years.

58

Tales from the Territory

There was never a dull moment, there were always plenty of characters to talk with, lots of humour and good times, but also many sad and tragic events.

Jimmy Stretton took over the job of station cook. The staff thought he was wonderful, especially after their experiences with the last cook, who'd been hopeless and seemed continually inebriated; we soon discovered that he'd been on the 'lemon essence', an alcoholic flavouring.

Jimmy was gay and proud of it. Within no time he'd revamped his bedroom with a frilly bedspread, lace curtains and feminine knick-knacks, and even a chandelier that he'd had sent up from Brisbane. He was a superb cook, as well as an excellent hairdresser and dressmaker. Every dish looked and tasted delicious.

I was used to cooking for my guests at home. But Jimmy would say, 'I'll send dinner over if you like. How many people?'

It was too easy to say yes. The kitchen girls would bring the food down and it would be put on the bain-marie until we were ready.

Mick Coombes, an old drover, was visiting Wave one Christmas and decided to drive over to Kelly's Camp, on Victoria River Downs Station. There, he and several men from the station celebrated the festive season, and may or may not have got on the grog. One partygoer, Danny Marr, a part-Aboriginal station employee, had gone to sleep in the long grass behind one of the vehicles—the owner of which, having no idea Danny was there, backed straight over his head.

The police were notified. Because the policeman and his wife were on their way to Victoria River Downs for Christmas dinner, Danny's body was placed in a body bag, brought back to the station and put in one of the vehicle sheds. After the policeman picked the body up and was on his way to Katherine, his vehicle broke down. By the time another vehicle was found and the body brought into town, it had taken hours and hours, and in *that* heat.

Another tragedy involved dear old Harry Selmes, one of the most extraordinary characters I met at Wave Hill. Harry was the brumby and donkey shooter for the Vesteys' Territory stations, and had been for many years. He camped in the bush, only coming to the station to renew his supplies, but having grown up in Sydney he was a gentleman in every way.

One day he knocked on our door. He'd come to see me.

He asked me if I would look after the gold watch that his parents had given him in 1935, for his twenty-first birthday.

Some months later, after a bushfire went through near Mataranka, Harry's body was found in his burnt-out vehicle. We'd lost a wonderful man.

Only very recently, I found out that after Harry's body was discovered in the early 1970s, his daughter came to collect his belongings. I didn't know this as it was many months before we heard through the grapevine that he had died.

Another time, coming back from Katherine, Ralph and I called in to the Top Springs roadhouse to get a cold softdrink for Penny. This would have been about 1975 or 1976. The publican said he had a problem and, knowing I was a nurse, asked if I could help. One of his Aboriginal customers had had a fight outside the hotel with his wife, hitting her so hard that the publican thought she was dead. Would I please take a look and confirm?

Going outside with the publican, leaving Ralph with Penny, I found the husband sitting in the dirt beside a seemingly life-less Aboriginal woman. 'She no good. She give me cheek. I bin hit him.' There appeared to be no remorse at what he had done. He allowed me to examine her as she lay there, in the dirt and her blood. Sadly, she was dead.

There was nothing more I could do, so the publican contacted the police and we left. On the news we heard talk of the murder but no sentence.

*

There was nothing sad about this next character. Mick Maloney from Brisbane was a great jovial guy who worked for Southern Cross Windmills and did most of his business with head office through Peter Morris or Roy Bell. But he was always there at the Katherine Show, where he attended the Brahman Dinner Dance with us.

In the sixties and seventies, everyone went to the Brahman Dinner Dance. Brahman beef was served as the main course. Brahman aren't as tasty as the British breeds, but they're tick resistant, which is a big plus in the North. These days, Brahman would be the major breed replacing the Shorthorn cattle of old. We didn't really care what meat we ate, as it was the people who made the dinner dances fun, all decked out in their formal gear and having a marvellous time together. Sadly there is no Brahman Dinner Dance anymore, so Mick tells me, but he recently went to his forty-ninth Katherine show. He only missed one show and the organisers of the dinner phoned him to ask him where he was. When he said he had the flu, they said 'But you should be here!' and had to admit that they'd organised a 'This is your life' event for him at the dinner.

59

The *Kookaburra*

It was strange how frequently the unexpected happened at Wave Hill. Early in my station life, I wasn't surprised to hear of the station's connection to one of Australia's longest-running aviation mysteries. This mystery, often spoken of around Wave, involved a Westland Widgeon aircraft, the *Kookaburra*, and its relationship to the Australian pioneering aviation hero Sir Charles 'Smithy' Kingsford Smith and his plane the *Southern Cross*.

After a historic flight from San Francisco to Sydney in 1928 by the *Southern Cross*, pilot Smithy and co-pilot Charles Ulm wanted more challenges, so they decided to fly to England. They were to refuel at Wyndham in the north of Western Australian, but they never arrived. 'We are about to make a forced landing in rough country,' was the last message received from the *Southern Cross* that day.

Scores of planes were soon frantically looking for Smithy and Ulm. However, attention would shortly be focused on another plane, the *Kookaburra*, piloted by Keith Anderson and carrying his mechanic, Bob Hitchcock.

Anderson was convinced that the search planes had been looking for Smithy in the wrong area. After hasty preparations, with no radio and a faulty compass, and short on provisions, the *Kookaburra* took off from Sydney on 4 April 1929. Engine trouble caused a forced landing in an area of loose sand and turpentine scrub in the Tanami Desert, 128 kilometres south-east of Wave.

Having managed to fix the engine, Anderson and Hitchcock found that the scrub was too thick to permit a take-off. Anderson had brought a pencil and wrote an account on the fabric of the *Kookaburra*'s rudder, describing the forced landing and their inability to take off again.

In a touch of irony, Anderson and Hitchcock were awaiting certain death from dehydration as Smithy and Ulm were found safe and well.

Planes were sent to search for the *Kookaburra* when it went missing. Lester Brain was the pilot who found the plane; he noted a body under the wing and dropped water. A ground search was mounted from Wave Hill, and thanks to three Aboriginal trackers—Banjo, Daylight and Tanami—after great difficulty the search party found the site and buried the two heroes. Later a party from Newcastle Waters Station arrived with coffins on board and removed the bodies, which were sent south to families for proper funeral services.

There was a propeller on display in the Wave Hill Station rec room, in perfect condition—a reminder of this race against time and fate. Apparently many of the search planes had landed at Wave Hill to refuel and collect supplies, such as the replacement propeller. I was told that it was meant as a replacement for one of the search aircraft, but had never been fitted, because the plane it had been intended for had met a fiery end. The burnt out remains of the plane were later transformed into a 'beef buggy', a small trailer for carting beef.

In later years, many unsuccessful attempts were made to again find the site of the *Kookaburra*. But Wave was about 16,000 square kilometres in size, with about half of this being unexplored desert country, with only one main road going through. Nearly fifty years passed and the location of the *Kookaburra* remained a mystery.

One morning in July 1976, I awoke to hear that Dick Smith and his party of *Kookaburra* searchers were amassed on the Wave Hill airstrip. Dick, one of Australia's best-known entrepreneurs and aviation adventurers, planned to write the last chapter of this historical quest. He had the money to do the job, but he was also working on a dream to find the plane that had gone in search of Smithy all those years ago.

On a preliminary trip in April, Dick had flown over Wave in a Twin Comanche with two friends, one a cameraman. July's *Kookaburra* expedition was much larger, and certainly well equipped: Dick had a huge four-wheel drive truck called a Unimog and about four or five other vehicles.

Soon after their arrival, Dick flew out to view the desert country in John Weymouth's helicopter. Upon landing, he walked only a few metres away and found, on turning, that he could no longer see the helicopter! One of Australia's most intrepid adventurers had lost his bearings. In that moment he could relate to the fear that Anderson and Hitchcock must have experienced.

Dick had talks with the Aboriginal people who'd been in the first search party. He hired the station grader together with its driver, Claypan. He graded a track down to what they called Anderson's Corner, where lines of longitude and latitude met on the map, south-east of Cattle Creek Station. But after five days of grid grading to ensure comprehensive searching out in the Tanami Desert, they still couldn't find the *Kookaburra*.

Dick had brought with him two memorial plaques: one to be left if they didn't find the *Kookaburra* and the other to be left at the site if they did. After placing the former, Dick and his party departed—but he was still determined that the desert was not going to win.

After those first visits, Dick contacted Lester Brain, the pilot who'd first found the *Kookaburra*. Dick discovered that a blowhole Lester had noted in 1929 was in a straight line with the *Kookaburra* and the Wave homestead.

The next year Dick returned, this time with his wife, Pip, his girls, Hayley and Jenny, and some of his experienced crew.

Following the directions Lester had given him, Dick, his family and team set out in Dick's helicopter with high hopes of achieving their objective. This time they were successful—they found the wreckage in the rough turpentine scrub of the Tanami Desert, 125 kilometres south-east of Wave Hill.

Standing around the burnt-out remains of the *Kookaburra*, there were mixed emotions. They were elated to find the plane but extremely saddened, too, as they viewed this symbolic reminder of the daring of those brave aviators. Dick later said, 'It was a moment to remember forever, a moment to dream about, to talk and laugh and cry about.'

On their return to the station, we gathered for a barbecue—part-celebration and part-hastily convened memorial service for the men of the *Kookaburra*.

As a result of this tragedy, compulsory planning of flights was introduced, so Anderson and Hitchcock did not die in vain. The remains of the *Kookaburra* were taken to Alice Springs where they are on display at the museum.

60

Where did we go wrong?

Education came to Wave Hill in 1961, when Ralph rounded up all the school-age children at the station and put them on the truck to take them to the settlement school. In 1976 these children, now adolescents, returned to Wave a few weeks before the Negri Races. They had completed their education at Kormilda College in Darwin.

Everyone, white and black, was busy preparing for the exciting event. The stock camps had taken the horses over several weeks before and were training them and setting up our campsites. On Monday the rest of the station travelled over to join them: truckloads of Aboriginal residents—including the adolescents, who usually missed out because they were away at school—and whites in their four-wheel drives, leaving a skeleton staff to hold the fort.

On arrival we settled in, unpacked, decided on meals for the day, and caught up with friends in the evening or just had a quiet night in our own camps. Everyone was so enthusiastic and looking forward to the rest of the week.

That same night the hawker vans arrived, and the proprietors started to set up their gear in preparation for Tuesday when trade would begin. This year there were three hawkers; they'd parked their vans in a row opposite the racecourse and hall. One was our friend Ben Humphreys.

After breakfast, Ralph took a truckload of workers down to the racing area to tidy up around the jockeys' room, the hall and the grandstand, and to put up the decorations. I went down sometime later with my baby daughter, Penny, and the new female bookkeeper from Wave Hill. We parked the car at the far entrance to the hall and then strolled along the avenue of hawker vans. There seemed to be quite a few people around but it didn't dawn on me until later that there were no Aboriginal women or children present. This was most unusual, as they all loved looking at the hawkers' merchandise.

Just in front of us as we strolled along was Leo, one of the white stockmen. Two Aboriginal youths came up and tried to pick a fight with him. Leo, a very easygoing fellow, just shrugged them off and said, 'Cut it out, you fellows. I don't want to fight with you.' But a third Aboriginal youth quickly joined them and they all started punching poor old Leo.

We were horrified and, racing across to the hall, I called frantically, 'Quick, Ralph, some of the blacks are picking on Leo. He's in trouble.'

Ralph and the other men, including tribal elders, ran out of the hall and looked over to the vans. A line of at least fifty young

Aboriginal people, a metre apart, were carrying fence pickets and marching towards us chanting, 'Fuckin' *cudia*, fuckin' *cudia*.' (*Cudia* meaning 'white man'.) I thought I was watching a western movie with the Indians attacking the cowboys!

'Hurry, Thea,' Ralph yelled, 'jump in the car, get up to Nicholson and tell the police in Wyndham.'

As we ran to the car, the bookkeeper said, 'Give me Penny while you open the door.' I handed her my daughter. Near the car, another mob of adolescents raced up to us. One young fellow, whom I'd known well and had fed as a child in the soup kitchen, threw a large rock that missed Penny by only a few inches.

Somehow, shocked as we were, we managed to get away and drive at speed to Nicholson. Len Hill, the manager, reported the incident to the police in Wyndham by two-way radio. Six policemen were immediately dispatched by plane to Nicholson and vehicles were made available for them to do their job. A few fights had broken out in some of the camps, but thankfully there were no injuries and everything settled down. Fortunately Leo came out of it okay.

The women were ready to go home from the Negri, but the men said, 'What's wrong with you? Of course we'll continue.' It's a man's world sometimes!

But it wasn't the same. Everyone—whites, Aboriginal elders and families—was very upset. Why had these adolescents acted in this way? Were they taught to hate whites at college, or did they hate the Vesteys? Maybe they were suffering like many adolescents today, who are unemployed, lack social support and have too much alcohol. These things can lead to extreme states of discouragement, and to rebel may seem to them to be their only option.

I guess we'll never know. All I know is that they ruined the best race meeting in the country that day.

61

Aboriginal customs

In 1976, Ralph received a letter from a guy who'd worked on the station about fifteen years before. This man had taken some sacred stones from a native burial place on Wave Hill and brought them with him to Queensland. He claimed his life had been hell since he'd committed this crime. His health had suffered, his wife had left him, one child had become very ill.

The sacred stones were already in the mail on their way to Wave when the letter arrived. The man wanted Ralph to return the stones to their rightful burial place, and Ralph was not happy. When the parcel arrived in the mailbag, he refused to go into the office. He sent Algie in to pick the parcel up, and then gave him a vehicle to take the *gudarji* back to where it belonged, or whichever sacred site the elders decided on.

One of the older Aboriginal men, Lightning, had come up to the hospital one time feeling weak and lethargic. I couldn't find anything wrong with him. I put him down on the list to see the doctor on his next visit. The girls sitting around the hospital said that Lightning had been 'sung'.

When the Aerial Medical Plane came, the doctor examined him and found nothing wrong, so they took him to Darwin for further examination and tests; again, nothing was found. He was sent home and died the week after.

Ralph believed in the Aboriginal superstitions. '*Gudarji*,' he would say, about pointing the bone or singing someone. 'Bad medicine.'

On Boxing Day 1978, Ralph took most of the station folk, white and Aboriginal, out to Seal Gorge on the Victoria River for a day of fishing and swimming. The area is very rocky with large amounts of scrub sweeping up from the river.

After a great day of swimming, fishing and barbecuing, it was time to leave. The troops were all mustered and were walking up the slope to our vehicles. But some of the Aboriginal people hadn't come with us. They were looking for Brisbane Sambo, who had disappeared.

Then the whole station started looking, in the gorges along the riverbank, up and around the hills, without success. According to his family, Brisbane Sambo knew that his time had come and, in the Aboriginal way, didn't wish to cause any fuss.

'Him bin gone, him bin finish,' the elders said.

The search continued until night fell, resuming again the next morning, but no trace of Brisbane Sambo was ever found.

62

Bidji Park

In 1976, Madeline and Milton left Gordon Downs and bought a property in the Brisbane Valley at Toogoolawah. I was envious of Madeline's accounts of pre-school meetings, parent–teacher evenings, sports days and football matches. Ralph and I had missed out on so much of our children's education.

We only went to end-of-school-year concerts at OLSH and St Joseph's every two years, when on holidays. There were no cheap flights in those days. Occasionally our boys would bring their mates home for holidays, or down south we'd have contact with their parents, going out to Pancakes on the Rocks, or Centrepoint restaurant, high up above the other city buildings. That was fun, but it wasn't the same as Madeline's day-to-day friendships with other parents in Queensland. Sometimes I did feel our isolation.

Each week I would read the *Queensland Country Life*, pouring over property sales. We and many of our friends wanted our own place in the country: to work for ourselves, but not too far from civilisation. How stupid we were—after living in the Territory, we could have made a life anywhere!

Ralph and I started looking at properties every holidays. It had to be in Queensland, but I'm not sure why we chose Queensland now; perhaps because it was cheaper and more countrified than New South Wales. While staying with Madeline and Milton one year, we found and bought a lush little property, with irrigation and good cultivation, on the hills just outside Toogoolawah. At first we couldn't think of what to name it, when Cudge suddenly said, 'Call it Bidji.' Penny, aged two, had been saying *bidji bidji* every time she looked at a bunch of grapes. Perhaps Penny had picked up the name 'bidji' from her Aboriginal nanny, Pansy. The Aboriginal people had a word that sounded like 'bidji' for some bush berries. But wherever Penny got that phrase from, we decided to call the property Bidji Park. It was a dairy to start with, but later we changed it over to a Murray Grey cattle stud.

When we first bought Bidji we employed a dairy farmer, went to a few dairy sales, managed to get a milk quota with Caboolture Dairy Association, and then went back to work at Wave. Gone were our extravagant holidays down south; our money went into sprucing up the rather dilapidated homestead at Bidji.

We were still committed to our life outback, though. Our friend Roger Steele, who was the Territorian government's Minister for Industrial Development, Overseas Trade, Primary Production and Fisheries, asked Ralph to become a board member of the

Northern Territory Development Corporation in Darwin in 1978. Its chairman was Noel Buntine, the man who'd brought road trains to the Territory. He did a lot for the Territory and in recognition of that they changed the name of the Buchanan Highway to the Buntine Highway.

Answering to Roger, the corporation looked at unusual development opportunities throughout the Territory that needed support, in some cases offering financial assistance when this was unavailable from the banks. Ralph was happy to join the board and enjoyed going to Darwin to assist with this very worthwhile venture.

One example of the work carried out was at the Rapid Flat roadhouse in the Tanami Desert—the most isolated roadhouse in Australia. It needed funds for a new lighting plant. These were unavailable from the banks, but the Northern Territory Development Corporation was able to help and prevent closure.

Times were changing. Some of our Vestey friends started leaving the north. Commitment to family was stronger than working for Lord Vestey. There were disturbances in the meat industry; meat workers going on strike for higher wages in the Vestey abattoir in Rockhampton, followed by rumours of Aboriginals marching on Vestey stations. It was a frightening time, especially after having experienced the riot at the Negri.

It was a difficult decision but in 1979 we decided to leave Wave Hill Station.

63

Leaving the Outback

After twenty-five years for Ralph, and twenty years for me, we left Wave Hill Station. Jenny and Dick Jansen took over the management. Dick was a nephew of Ray Jansen of Limbunya.

Jimmy Stretton held a 'silver service' lunch for us down at Five Mile Creek. We either drove down or rode the horses. As usual, the food and drinks were served beautifully. It was great fun.

After a big farewell party in the rec room the following day, I took photos of all my Aboriginal staff. We felt sad leaving them all. What did their future hold without Ralph's guidance?

Then we headed off. Ralph was putting on a brave face. I'm sure he hated leaving, but he never actually said so.

Not only did we have our dairy farm at Bidji to go to, but we'd also bought the corner store in Toogoolawah to generate cash flow until the farm got on its feet. We still had three children at boarding school, now at Downlands College in Toowoomba, much closer than Sydney.

*

Did we miss the Northern Territory? At first I think we were so busy with our farm, the shop, our children and making a new life that we didn't have time to think about it. We had our Territory mates, the Fulchers and the Dorans, living not far away, with whom we could open up, compare problems, relax and enjoy great company. Without them we wouldn't have survived so well.

Thank goodness we sold the shop after two years, two months and three days of being storekeepers. It was the worst thing we ever did. Only two days off a year; working from 6.30 a.m. to 6.30 p.m. seven days a week; having to deal with overly demanding customers. I think people need to be born into the retail trade before they take on a corner store.

We spent ten years at Toogoolawah before we sold Bidji Park and moved to the Darling Downs, which was more like the undulating hills of Wave. The country was also much more to our liking, but we missed the lifetime friends we'd made in the Brisbane Valley.

We purchased a grazing block near Oakey, which we named Murrawah after Ralph's Aboriginal nanny. We'd started showing our stud Murray Grey cattle quite successfully when in Toogoolawah, so that continued on the Downs until the big drought came in 1992, when we had to sell all our stock.

Throughout our years in Queensland, Ralph and I continued to catch up with our Territory friends at dinner parties, at our holiday house on North Stradbroke Island, and at the yearly Territory Reunion at the Olsens' home at Beerwah. I'd never met the Olsens before this; they had been managing property on the Barkely tablelands.

Ralph was much loved by his family and friends. He often had some friend ringing him up to have a chat—he didn't need to ring them because they would always ring him. He told the most incredible stories of life on the stations, and I never heard the same one twice. He drew people to him, although at first he was always shy.

In 1989, Ralph became ill and was diagnosed with lung cancer. The surgeon at the Wesley Hospital removed a small part of Ralph's lung, which contained the cancer in two small capsules. Ralph battled to give up smoking, but unfortunately his habit was too strong and the cancer returned.

In July 1992, the Vestey Company sold its properties at a sale in Brisbane, which we attended. This brought to a close the Vestey family's involvement in the Northern Australian cattle industry.

On 3 February 1995, with the whole family present—including Madeline and Milton—Ralph passed peacefully away a few hours after his fifty-ninth birthday, which had been celebrated in St Vincent's Hospital, Toowoomba.

64

Murrawah

At Ralph's funeral in Toowoomba, our old friend John Kirsh—who had worked in the mission town of Balgo—gave the eulogy, telling a story about Ralph that I'd never heard before.

I'd met Murrawah, Ralph's tribal mother, and had assumed that she was more a nanny than a mum. But here is the story of Murrawah.

In the mid-1930s, Ralph's parents, Dick and Mary Hayes, had a farm at Pretty Bend in Queensland. In 1936 they accepted a management position with the Vesteys at Waterloo Station in the Northern Territory. (Waterloo is east of the Ord River Scheme, where the famous Argyle Station was found and pioneered by Patrick Durack, as written about by Mary Durack in her book *Kings in Grass Castles*.) Mary and Dick brought with them their first-born son, Ralph, who was a tiny baby having been born prematurely in Brisbane on 2 February 1936.

The move must have been very hard for Mary who, although a champion horse rider, had been brought up in Brisbane. Her new life on an outback property with a baby was isolating, especially when her loving husband had to spend a lot of his time in the stock camp, mustering cattle and fencing.

There were only a handful of Aboriginal people at Waterloo, employed around the homestead or in the stock camp. Ralph was loved by this group of nomadic people, none of whom had their own children. Most likely they had never seen a white baby before.

Mary had Aboriginal help with the cooking, housework and gardening, and she employed a young Aboriginal woman, about the same age as herself, to look after baby Ralph. Her name was Murrawah.

When Mary was leaving for Wyndham to have Lynn, her second child, she asked Murrawah to look after Ralph. Little Ralph fretted for his mother. He became very distressed and quite ill. Murrawah took the tiny child to her breast. She loved this child as if he were her own. Although she wasn't pregnant and had never been with child, she produced milk and suckled Ralph with all the love that she could give him, and he survived.

Thanks to Murrawah, Ralph lived and the story in this book was possible.

Before Ralph and I left Wave Hill to go south, Murrawah— who had moved from Waterloo to Kalkaringi, the renamed Aboriginal settlement at Wave—came to visit. There was a knock on the homestead's laundry door. Cudge—Mary— was also visiting; she went to answer it. There stood Murrawah.

'Good day, Murrawah, what are you doing here?' Cudge asked.

Murrawah

'I've come to see my son.'

'Who is your son?'

'Dat Ralph, he bin my son.'

'Ralph is my son, not yours.'

'No, Missus, you bin born him, but me bin grow him up. He my son.'

Epilogue

In July 2010 I found myself again on the road to Wave Hill.

This time it was with my new partner, Bob, whom I'd met while I was living on North Stradbroke Island.

I'd always wanted to go back some day, and I wanted to show Bob what had been such a big part of my life. Also there were three people from my Wave Hill days whom I desperately wanted to see: Emilie, Algie and Pansy.

Before we left on our trip to the Territory, I wrote to the owners of Wave, the Oxenfords, to ask if we could visit the station. Not having received a response, we rang from Top Springs—and yes, were relieved to hear that we were very welcome to come.

I was so excited as we drove into the station on the dirt road, passing Five Mile Creek where Jimmy had put on our silver service lunch. The buildings came into view as we rounded the curve in the road. Instead of us passing the old garage, there on the right was a huge vehicle shed. The weather station was no longer near the top cottage, but I found out later it had been moved nearer to the homestead; the manager's wife still did the weather. It was amazing: the other buildings hadn't changed, but the trees we'd planted were now ten metres high.

Epilogue

Greg and Alison Daikin, the managers, made us very welcome. Alison was fascinated by everything about Wave, because there seemed to be no photos or history of the station anywhere when they'd taken over.

They took us out to the old station to see if I could put a plan down of the position of the various buildings, as there was nothing left except a few sheets of iron, chunks of old cement and a bit of scrub. Even the road was in a different position. You could see the cement outline of the Aboriginal houses, and I found a small section of ant bed where the tennis court must have been. I also found the grave of the unknown child, thought to be the offspring of a Wave manager many years before. Other than that, I recognised nothing, and yet the memory of the old station is firmly implanted on my mind. It was sad going back there.

At the current station drinks were served in the rec room around the old bar where we met some of the staff. The propeller from 1929 was still hanging on the wall! There were only two Aboriginal employees, both stockmen.

We ate in the old dining room where everything was the same, including the smoko area. The main difference I noted was the lack of domestic and gardening staff. The overseer's wife looked after the gardens, and everyone did their own washing. Gosh, we were spoilt in our time, but then it gave us more time for the more important jobs we had to do.

The overseer offered to take us on the bore run, but not in a truck—we went by plane. Wow! We flew over about ten bores, noted the start of a bushfire at the side of the Buntine Highway, and enjoyed looking over the beautiful undulating Downs country.

The next day we drove down to Daguragu to find my old house girls, Emilie and Pansy. Driving into this community was quite daunting: there were large squares of unkempt grass and scrub surrounded by old prefabricated houses.

We saw an Aboriginal man carrying a child in his arms; the child looked limp and lifeless. Stopping, we started to get out of the car to talk to him, to offer help. He waved us on and disappeared between the houses. Was there a medical clinic there? We felt powerless!

Driving on, we saw a group of people sitting in the yard. I jumped out of the car to ask if there were any former Wave employees here. 'Yes,' I was told, 'up dere, dat house alonga dere.' We mentioned the sick child but they just shook their heads, making no comments.

Arriving at the house, I walked through the gateway. Three Aboriginal people were sitting in the dirt; a dead dog lay two metres away.

'You fella from that Wave Hill?' I said.

'Yes, Missus,' they replied.

'Me Missus Ralph,' I said.

'Ah Missus, Missus Ralph,' they cried as they rushed to embrace me. Hugging and kissing ensued from Connie, who must have been eighty-odd, with her hair dyed black; Oscar, a great old stockman; and Iris, who was only a child when I'd last seen her.

Bob entered the yard and couldn't believe his eyes at the jubilant cries from the three, and the hugging and kissing that went on.

They told me that Emilie and Algie had died. I was shocked.

'Where that Pansy?' I asked.

'Pansy at Kalkaringi,' they informed me.

We were about to leave when Iris said, 'Missus, don't go yet, dat social club him been open soon. We get drink. We no money. You buy.'

At Kalkaringi we found Pansy, Biddy, Topsy and Cushion.

Once again a group gathered, screaming with delight when I said, 'Me Missus Ralph.'

Pansy had hardly changed. She was so happy to see me. She'd been like a nanny to Penny, always there if I had to shoot down to the hospital, or was called to the office for a radiophone call.

Pansy loved my children: 'How dat Anthony, Harji, Jason and little Penny?' she asked. 'They got him Aboriginal skin name—"Jubuda", dat name.'

Biddy decided she was going to be our guide. We had to make room in the front of the vehicle for the three of us, before going on a tour to visit more of my old friends: Ida and her husband, Rankin; Mary Anne; and Marian, who'd had the twins. We then stopped at the Kalkaringi store to purchase a few things.

Word had got around that Missus Ralph was here. People, young and old, kept coming up to me. 'Missus, 'member me?'

'You bin give me my name, "Norman".' 'My mother alonga me, Ena.' 'Missus, me Toby.' And so it went on.

Bob and I, last year, went to the Wave Hill/Jinparrak/Canberra Exchange Art Exhibition in Canberra and caught up with now famous indigenous artists Biddy and Jimmy Wave Hill. They were ecstatic to see us again. Bob mentioned the stock camp at Wave Hill to Jimmy.

At the mention of Wave Hill and the stock camp, Jimmy's eyes lit up. 'Bob, working in dat stock camp, riding dem horses, doin' dat big muster. Dem were the good day.'

When Bob and I had visited them back in 2010, I had wondered how they felt living where they lived now, not being on a cattle station having their jobs, being involved in running a great cattle station.

'You fella happy?' I had asked them.

'Yes, Missus. We got im air-conditioned house.'

I wondered if they were really happy. Do they still think of the Dreamtime; the corroboree; the life in the stock camp; mustering the cattle; telling stories around the campfire; these great stockmen, now with nothing to do?

And my housegirls who'd always been part of the family, who were always there at important occasions, and digging yams with the children, teaching them about bush tucker, being teased by the stockmen. What is their life like now, in their air-conditioned houses? The young people having no jobs; drinking too much; forgetting their Aboriginal culture. Working for Vesteys they had their jobs and they also had the freedom to continue their culture.

But I do know that Ralph loved these people as they loved him, and besides very successfully running Wave Hill Station and Gordon Downs, he was also a paternal figure to these Aboriginal people. He was someone with whom they could discuss problems in their own language, share stories, tell jokes; and he helped them as much as he possibly could.

As for me, I was so proud to be beside Ralph in our initiation as a young overseer and a naive young nurse, later to manage one of the largest cattle stations in Australia. My serious concerns about going to the Outback as a young nurse were resolved within a week of arrival. I was fascinated by Wave Hill from the moment I arrived. I seemed to fit in, this city girl, this world traveller, this adventurer. I loved my work looking after the health of these wonderful Aboriginal people, and the white staff took some beating, too. We had a wonderful life and a beautiful family.

This whim to have an interview for a job just to see a cattle station turned out to be the greatest adventure of my life.

Acknowledgements

My sincere thanks to Jane Grieve who told Mark Lewis at Allen & Unwin that I had an interesting story.

To Kerrie Ross, my fabulous tutor at the 'Writing for Pleasure' course at Narrandera TAFE; Sharon Farlow for help with the poem; and my fellow students for help and encouragement. Thank you all.

To Claire Kingston, my publisher at Allen & Unwin, I am eternally grateful, and to the rest of the team there, thank you all. I am so lucky to have my story recognised and published by this great team of caring professional people.

To Freda Marnie Nichols, thank you for dragging out my thoughts, feelings and for expanding my book.

To my friends who had to put up with emails and telephone calls to confirm different aspects of my story—Tony Clark, Ces Watts, Len Hill, Robyn and Graham Fulcher, Jos Doran, Roger Steele, Gavin MacDonald, Mick Maloney, Madeline and Milton Hayes, Molly and Basil Courts, Tony Guerner, Jock Bremnar, Alan Johnson, Clive Ringler, Anna Underwood, Dorothy Sing and Terry Underwood.

To my three sons, Anthony, David (Harji), and Jason, star players in my book.

And to another star, my daughter, Penny, and to son-in-law, Patrick Joyce, for your support and legal advice.

And to Bob Black, my partner, who has had to make his own cuppa, make his own lunch, listen to the latest chapter, all while working hard on the property. I couldn't have done it without you.

Thank you all.